Photograph of Gustave Moreau
at about age forty
◄

Gustave Moreau

Julius Kaplan

Published by the
Los Angeles County Museum of Art
and
New York Graphic Society

Library of Congress
Catalog Card Number 74-76953
Copyrighted © 1974 by
Museum Associates of the
Los Angeles County Museum of Art
All rights reserved
ISBN 87587-059-7 (paperbound)
ISBN 0-8212-0628-1 (clothbound)

Published by the
Los Angeles County Museum of Art
Clothbound edition published by
New York Graphic Society,
Greenwich, Connecticut 06830

Exhibitions:
Los Angeles County Museum of Art
July 23 — September 1, 1974
California Palace of the
Legion of Honor
September 14 — November 3, 1974

Contents

Acknowledgments	6
Preface	7
Introduction	7
Chronology	9
Early Works	11
The 1860s	22
The 1870s and 1880s	34
Religious Subjects	43
Fables	46
Late Works	50
The Exhibition	59
Catalog	127
Appendix I: The Fables of La Fontaine	139
Appendix II: Moreau's Commentaries	141
Bibliography	145

Acknowledgments

I would like to take this opportunity to thank the many people who have made this exhibition possible. First, my sincere gratitude to Jean Paladilhe, Curator of the Moreau Museum, who aided me from the very beginning of my research and whose cooperation was essential to this exhibition. Charles Millard, Curator of Nineteenth-Century European Art at the Los Angeles County Museum, responded enthusiastically to the idea of the Moreau exhibition, and his constant support was vital to this project. I also wish to thank Kenneth Donahue and Ian White, the Directors of the participating museums, and Lanier Graham, Chief Curator at the Palace of the Legion of Honor, for their positive reception of the exhibition. To all lending institutions and private collectors, to the staffs at both the Los Angeles County Museum of Art and the Palace of the Legion of Honor, my great debt is hereby acknowledged. However, five people must be singled out for their special efforts. Paul Bittler, guardian of the Moreau Museum, was an indispensable helper. Jeanne Doyle, Coordinator of Exhibitions and Publications of the Los Angeles County Museum of Art, and her staff: Joanne Jaffe, Lilli Cristin, and Diane Stutts were steady allies in bringing this exhibition and catalog to their present form. So, too, were the Museum's Registrar, Patricia Nauert, and her assistants. Finally, I am profoundly grateful to my wife, Robin, for having served as reader and editor of the many drafts that preceded this catalog and for her stimulating questions which often penetrated to the core of basic issues.

Gustave Moreau's reputation has grown considerably since the retrospective held at the Louvre in 1961, and throughout Europe and Japan there have been almost annual showings devoted to his work. Yet, in the United States there has been only one Moreau exhibition and that was shared with two other artists.[1] The present showing therefore, represents the first exhibition in America devoted exclusively to Moreau.

Prior to the 1960s the basis for Moreau's fame was that he had been the teacher of Matisse and the Fauves. It was this association and the esteem the Surrealists had for him, rather than his own artistic achievement, that kept his name from the oblivion which had befallen so many of his nineteenth-century colleagues. But the evaluation of Moreau's place in the history of modern art remained problematic. Although in recent exhibitions he has been interpreted as a Symbolist,[2] or a precursor of the Surrealists,[3] or even as a proto-Abstract Expressionist,[4] such interpretations result from focusing on only a part of his art. Following the example of von Holten[5] and the Louvre retrospective he organized a decade ago, this exhibition will examine the entirety of Moreau's artistic interests.

Moreau's pictures and writings furnish the basic documentation for this study that has made extensive use of the riches of Gustave Moreau Museum in Paris. Formally recognized as a museum by the French government in 1902, this collection makes it possible to study the full range of the artist's artistic and intellectual life. A four-story structure built around the smaller house where Moreau lived from 1854 till his death, the museum contains — in addition to oil paintings, watercolors, drawings, and sculpture -- Moreau's books, notes, the letters he received, as well as such personal artifacts as clothing and family pictures.

This study, an outgrowth of my dissertation,[6] reflects my own interpretation of the known facts and is intended to be the first thorough examination of Moreau in English covering the main phases of his career. However, when all the drawings in the Moreau Museum and letters in private hands are made available for study, there will be much work to be done. The nature of exhibitions and the difficulty of borrowing art works makes it impossible to include some of the examples of Moreau's work which are most important in terms of his historical development. Hence, to be both lucid and comprehensive, the catalog has had at times to go beyond the content of the exhibition.

Moreau's historical importance lies in the special position he occupied between academic and avant-garde painting. As a student at the Ecole des Beaux-Arts, he learned to create carefully drawn and precisely finished works based upon studies from nature (the model), the Old Masters, and subjects from ancient history, mythology, and religion. Such academic elements are apparent throughout his oeuvre and were recognized by his contemporaries, who elected him to official honors culminating in a membership in the French Academy.[7] But even as a student he was attracted to the Academy's antithesis: the romantic art of Delacroix. Following Delacroix's example, Moreau painted such scenes as contemporary horsemen engaged in dramatic action and subjects taken from Shakespeare. The apparent contradiction which existed in Moreau's art also became evident later in his teaching at the Ecole des Beaux-Arts. There, he not only sponsored students who were otherwise unacceptable to the Academy with its then rigid standards of judgment, but even encouraged students with blatantly anti-academic styles (Matisse, for instance) to follow their own predilections.[8]

Moreau was not only able to bridge the academic and the avant-garde, he also was an intermediary between Romanticism and Symbolism. Throughout his career he worked in a great variety of styles, achieving a broad artistic vocabulary, a stylistic completeness that is one of the salient ingredients of Romanticism.[9] In this sense then, he was a Romantic painter, as he was when he chose to concentrate on themes revolving around characters from mythology or the Bible, whether involved in struggles against physical passion or shown in moments of contemplation. By the end of his career, however, his paintings and his statements about them paralleled characteristics of late nineteenth-century Symbolism. For example, he believed that the meaning of a painting resides in its color and line and becomes evident when a spectator contemplates the picture.

Moreau synthesized elements from academic, Romantic, and Symbolist art because his motive for painting combined the basic goals of these movements: to find both a personal and universal meaning in life. The particular manner in which he synthesized these elements separates him from Realism, Naturalism, and Impressionism — the major avant-garde currents in nineteenth-century art. The objective of these latter movements was to record nature as directly as possible — an artistic goal which ran counter to Moreau's more philosophical aim. But, he could not completely escape the positivism prompting his society's belief that art should provide an accurate image of nature. Albeit indirectly, his art, too, responds to the positivism of his age.

A constant element in Moreau's art is its sexual content, and some writers suggest that latent homosexuality may be at its core.[10] However, those closest to Moreau, his ex-student and companion Henri Rupp, and Georges Rouault, who was the first curator of the Moreau Museum, always testified to the normalcy of Moreau's private life. Although they may have been interested in protecting his reputation, their assertions have achieved greater credibility since his twenty-five-year relationship with Adelaide-Alexandrine Dureux (1837-1890) has been uncovered.[11] It is true that Moreau never married her, and their relationship may conceivably have been a platonic one. Nor does the existence of this long attachment necessarily negate the idea that his paintings were simply sublimations of repressed homosexuality. However, it does suggest the possibility that sublimation played no greater role in Moreau's art than it does in that of any artist.

Throughout the following essay I use general art historical terms, such as Romanticism. Because the meanings of such terms are subject to debate, and vagueness can result, I will attempt consistent working definitions. The use of these terms is inescapable, for they help explain the general changes in cultural expression that form the context for Moreau's production. And, because Moreau is a perfect example of an artist who mixed together contradictory cultural components, the shades of meaning and shifts of emphasis which occupied him are understandable only within the context of the art movements of his time.

This catalog and exhibition participate in the current reevaluation of nineteenth-century art which attempts to establish a proper historical perspective on the period. As a result of the diversity of the art produced during this time, it has become impossible to accept completely the traditional interpretation that during this age there was a logical progression of revolutionary movements. The stylistic development which began with Courbet and extended from Manet to the present does not reflect the whole course of the period. Even the important paintings of the dominant avant-garde cannot be understood fully if removed from the total context in which they occurred. This study of Moreau's work, then, hopefully will serve as a step in the direction of establishing a proper historical perspective for this period by focusing on two forces: the specific political, social, intellectual, and artistic climate of France during Moreau's lifetime and his individual and unique artistic character.

Chronology

1826
Born in Paris on April 6, son of Louis-Jean Marie Moreau (1790-1862) and Adèle Pauline Desmoutier (1802-1884).

1835-39
Studies at the Collège Rollin, Paris, and wins drawing prize on August 20, 1839.

1841
Summer trip to Italy — Turin, Milan, Parma, Pisa, Florence, Genoa — with his mother, aunt, and uncle. A sketchbook from this trip is preserved in the Moreau Museum.

1846
Enters the Ecole des Beaux-Arts, Paris, in October, as a student of François Edouard Picot (1786-1868).

1848
Fails at first attempt at Prix de Rome.

1849
Fails at second attempt at Prix de Rome. A period of government commissions begins, and he is asked to copy Annibale Carracci's *Virgin of the Cherries* for 800 francs.

1851
Receives government commission of 600 francs for his *Pietà*. Begins close friendship with the painter, Théodore Chasseriau (1819-1856). They are neighbors when Moreau lives on the rue Laval, avenue Frochot 28.

1852
Participates for the first time in a Salon Exhibition with the *Pietà* (No. 935), which shows the strong influence of Delacroix. *Song of Songs* commissioned by the government for 2,000 francs.

1853
Exhibits *Song of Songs* in the Salon (No. 846) along with *Darius, Fleeing After the Battle of Arbelles, Stops, Exhausted, to Drink in a Pond* (No. 847). Both show influence of Delacroix and Chasseriau. At this time Moreau lives with his parents at 16 rue des Trois Frères.

1854
The *Athenians Delivered to the Minotaur in the Labyrinth on Crete* commissioned by the government for 4,000 francs. Moreau and his parents move to 14 rue de la Rochefoucauld, the location of the present Moreau Museum.

1855
The *Athenians* (No. 3703) exhibited in the Universal Exhibition. Moreau begins his correspondence with the painter and writer Eugène Fromentin. Although they communicate throughout their lives, the most important exchange of letters ends in 1862.

1856
Delacroix writes a favorable note about Moreau in his journal on October 10 after seeing him at Chasseriau's death bed.

1857
Makes a second trip to Italy; spends March in Rome; Summer in Florence; August in Milan and Lugano where he meets his parents; Fall to December in Venice. Winter and Spring of 1859 in Florence; Rome in May, Summer in Naples where he makes friends with Elie Delaunay, Leon Bonnat, Chapu, Emile and Henri Levy, and Degas. (Among his circle of friends in Paris at this time were Antoine Koenigswarter, Alexandre Destouches, Eugène Lacheurié, Amedée Cantaloube, Frédéric de Courcy, Armand du Mesnil, Joseph Tourny, and Narcisse Berchère.)

1861
Begins developing important new style in *Oedipus and the Sphinx*.

1862
Paints a *Chemin de Croix* for the Church at Decazeville. His father dies.

1864
First inclusion of his work in a Salon exhibition since 1855, shows *Oedipus and the Sphinx* (No. 1388). Wins medal and achieves first major critical acclaim.

1865
Continues new mature style with *Jason* (No. 1539), *Young Man and Death* (No. 1540). Both in the Salon. Wins medal. Begins twenty-five year relationship with Adelaide-Alexandrine Dureux. Received by the court at Compiègne in November.

1866
Several works included in the Salon: two oils, *Orpheus* (No. 1404) and *Diomedus* (No. 1405). The former purchased by the government for 8,000 francs. Also exhibits two drawings, *Hesiod visited by a Muse* (No. 2430) and a *Peri* (project for an enamel) (No. 2431).

1867
Exhibits *Young Man and Death* (No. 484), *Orpheus* (No. 485) in the *Universal Exhibition*.

1869
Two oils, *Prometheus* (No. 1746) and *Europe* (No. 1747), included in the Salon along with two watercolors, *Pietà* (No. 2989) and *The Saint and the Poet* (No. 2990). Wins medal but is criticized by members of the press.

1870-1871
Remains in the city during the Siege of Paris (Franco-Prussian War).

1874
Refuses request to decorate the Chapel of the Virgin in the Church of St. Genevieve (The Pantheon).

1875
Named Chevalier of the Legion of Honor.

1876
First appearance in the Salon since 1869. His new style apparent in two oils, *Hercules and the Hydra of Lerna* (No. 1505) and *Salome* (No. 1506), one watercolor, *Apparition* (No. 2774); and *St. Sebastian*, distemper wash and wax, from the Lepel-Cointet collection.

1878
Moreau's exhibited works in the *Universal Exhibition* include oils: *Hercules and the Hydra of Lerna* (No. 656), *Salome* (No. 657), *Jacob and the Angel* (No. 658), *David* (No. 659), *Moses on the Nile* (No. 660), *The Defeated Sphinx* (No. 661); and watercolors: *Apparition* (No. 1011), *Phaeton* (project for a decoration) (No. 1012), *Salome Carrying the Head of John the Baptist* (No. 1013), a *Massier* (No. 1014), a *Peri* (No. 1015). Wins 2nd class medal.

1879
Commissioned by Anthony Roux to work on the Fables of La Fontaine.

1880
Last appearance in the Salon with *Galatea* (No. 2711) and *Helen* (No. 2712).

1881

Exhibition of Fables; Moreau's twenty-five interpretations highly praised. Roux asks him to continue work on this commission.

1882

Begins enlarging earlier works.

1883

Made Officier of the Legion of Honor.

1884

Achieves notoriety as a result of the publication of Huysmans' *A Rebours*. Mother dies.

1885

Makes trip to Belgium and Holland.

1886

Exhibition of sixty-three Fables of La Fontaine at the Galerie Goupil. During this year he also exhibits *Persian Poet, Sacred Lake, Ganymede, Victorious Sphinx, Salome in Prison, The Poet's Complaints*. Begins a business association with the dealer, J. Montaignac, which lasts until 1891, allowing collectors to purchase his works.

1888

Elected member of the Académie des Beaux-Arts of the Institute de France in November.

1889

Begins work on his last large finished oil, *Jupiter and Semele*. Finishes it in 1895.

1890

Reads his notice on M. G. Boulanger at the Académie des Beaux-Arts on November 22. Death of Adelaide-Alexandrine Dureux (1837-1890).

1892

Succeeds his friend Elie Delaunay as Professor at the Ecole des Beaux-Arts. Begins his career as a teacher of such artists as Matisse and Rouault.

1893

Begins a series of business transactions with the firm of Allard & Noel, making his new work available for purchase.

1894

On June 12 cartoon ordered for the Gobelin Tapestry Works for 10,000 francs. Moreau finishes it in 1896.

1895

Moreau's two-story home remodeled into four-story structure it is today to create a museum to house his works. The construction finished in 1896.

1898

Dies of stomach cancer in Paris on April 18.

1902

The State accepts his home as the Musée Gustave Moreau.

Moreau's future development grew from his activities of the 1840s and 1850s, a period devoted to study and experimentation.[12] By the age of thirteen his talent was recognized when he won an award for draftsmanship as a student at the Collège Rollin.[13] The drawing was probably a copy of an engraving or a study of a plaster cast.[14] Although the prize-winning example does not figure among them, the earliest of Moreau's works known to us are preserved in the Moreau Museum. They include a sketchbook from his trip to Italy in the summer and fall of 1841, and from 1842 watercolors of genre scenes with figures dressed in seventeenth-century costume. These works reveal his talent but do not show his originality since they simply follow the normal practices of nineteenth-century anecdotal drawing.

By the mid 1840s Moreau's parents, recognizing their son's talent for painting, sought expert advice on a career for him in art. They showed his work to the painter, Dedreux-Dorcy, whose favorable response can be considered the starting point of Moreau's artistic life.[15] Even before Moreau passed the entrance examination for the Ecole des Beaux-Arts on October 7, 1846, he began his studies as a private student in the studio of François Edouard Picot (1786-1868), a well-known artist and an instructor at the Ecole. While in Picot's studio, Moreau painted academic studies of single nude figures (see fig. 1), copied the Old Masters (cat. no. 2), and produced some oil sketches as well as large, finished paintings. Central to academic instruction was the idea that an artist learned from the study of the great art of the past, and this concept left its mark on Moreau throughout his career.

In 1848, at the age of twenty-two, Moreau competed for the highest honor awarded to a French art student, the Prix de Rome. Subsidized by the French Government, this prize entitled the recipient to a four-year scholarship in Rome. Moreau's first attempt failed, as did his second the following year when the prescribed subject was "Ulysses recognized by his nurse Eurycleia." Moreau's finished *Ulysses* does not survive today, but his fluid oil sketch preserves his composition of this subject (cat. no. 3). Two of his preparatory drawings (cat. nos. 4 and 5) with their subtle gradations of light and dark show Moreau's interest in the way light plays over the forms. Similarly, they are characteristic of academic preparatory studies in their concern with contour and the linear definition of anatomical and other detail, such as drapery folds. The canvas by Boulanger that won the 1849 prize gives a sense of the characteristics shared by all the pictures entered in this competition: careful draftsmanship, the inclusion of a variety of physical types of different ages and with different expressions, and a knowledge of history, literature, and archaeology (fig. 2). Both Moreau and Boulanger knew that the academy judges would be impressed if they "quoted" from some respected example of past art, and both apparently based their compositions on Flaxman's version of this scene which has the actors in roughly the same positions.[16]

Having lost the competition a second time, Moreau left Picot's studio and renounced his desire to win the Prix de Rome. Turning away from the pursuit of such academic honors, instead he sought recognition for his work through public exhibitions. The influence of his father, an architect for the city of Paris and the Ministry of the Interior, won him some small government commissions,[17] one of which was the first work

he exhibited, a *Pietà* shown in the Salon of 1852.[18] We know how this last painting looked from the only engraving Moreau ever created (cat. no. 6). Favorably reviewed by the critics Edmond and Jules de Goncourt, the *Pietà* was praised for the emotional quality of the figures, and for its solid harmony and striking effect.[19] Such a response to the first public exposure of his work must have encouraged Moreau, although one critic considered him excessively influenced by the art of Delacroix.[20]

Obviously Moreau was attracted to Delacroix when he sought an alternative to the style which had failed to gain him the Prix de Rome. No doubt this attraction was the starting point for the Romantic current that runs through his subsequent work. A painting of a horseman, one of several similar scenes from this period in the Moreau Museum, is full of Romantic elements typical of Delacroix (cat. no. 7). Its subject, a red-coated figure on a horse caught in the middle of a leap, is typically Romantic, as are the painting's dark pigmentation and thick impasto. Even when Moreau was most strongly influenced by Delacroix, his academic background continued to make its presence felt. Turning to scenes from Shakespeare, a sign of the anglomania that generally characterized Romantic art, he did a number of subjects from *Hamlet*. In one of two drawings, which were engraved by his friend Narcisse Berchère in 1854, Moreau selected for illustration one of the most dramatic moments in the play, the poisoning of the king (cat. no. 8). Despite the violence of the scene depicted and the agitated contours of the forms — evident in much of the draftsmanship both of Delacroix and Moreau's close friend, Chasseriau — Moreau used a shallow space and triangular structure to impose an almost classical order upon the compositions. The result is a stability which would have pleased his teacher, Picot. Such careful ordering is a sign that the lessons he had learned from the Ecole were not forgotten.

There is no doubt that Moreau also knew the work of Ingres, the only contemporary French master whose reputation rivaled that of Delacroix, though it is not clear exactly when Moreau made his copy of the Ingres portrait drawing (cat. no. 1). This, however, is the only example of a direct contact with Ingres, whose influence on Moreau was transmitted to him indirectly through his friend Chasseriau. A student of Ingres, Chasseriau greatly admired Delacroix, and he synthesized the contradictory stylistic elements — line and color — of the two older artists.[21] The result was a unique and essentially Romantic art — melancholy, sensual, and at times monumental.

It can even be said that for a time Moreau was under Chasseriau's spell. In the early 1850s they were neighbors,[22] and in 1853 Chasseriau gave Moreau some drawings, three of which hang in the Moreau Museum today. The style of many of Moreau's notebook sketches (figs. 3 and 4) is wholly that of Chasseriau. Indeed, this was Moreau's first close exposure to an active, talented artist able to introduce him to a means of making his art a synthesis of unlike tendencies — a process which occupied him throughout his career.

Moreau's penchant for a fluid Romantic style, as well as for Romantic subjects, continued throughout his lifetime. His large *Song of Songs* in Dijon and *Darius Fleeing after the Battle of Arbelles, Stops Exhausted, to Drink in a Pond,* both in the Salon of 1853, represent the apex of his Romanticism with their agitated movement and drama created by thick, fluid, and colorful pigmentation (fig. 5 and cat. no. 9).[23] In the case of Moreau's *Herald* (cat. no. 10), a decorative and vibrant watercolor, the subject is taken from the Renaissance. This kind of reference to the Renaissance is a typical Romantic device, intended to glorify the past and thereby escape the banality of the present.

If Moreau was consistently influenced by Romanticism, there were times when he had to fight its hold on him. In the 1850s he had to face increasing criticism that his art was too closely modeled after that of Delacroix.[24] In response to this criticism his style underwent a transformation which is evident in *The Athenians Delivered to the Minotaur in the Labyrinth on Crete* (cat. no. 11), 1855. Although the finished painting and some of the preliminary drawings for it (cat. nos. 12 and 13) contain the same anatomical exaggerations found in Moreau's previous work (cf. *Song of Songs*), they are less theatrical, more reserved. The *Athenians'* thick impasto, visible brushstrokes, and summary rendering, the contorted postures of the figures with their wind-blown hair and drapery are all reminiscent of Delacroix. However, there is also a movement away from Delacroix in the refinement of physical types, in the expansion of the composition which creates quieter rhythms across the canvas, and in the more precise linear definition apparent in such details as the drapery. In addition, Moreau has lit the picture more evenly than previous works and has employed more widely differentiated hues. Moreau's attempt to shake off Delacroix's influence also led him away from the kind of subject matter generally associated with the latter's "Romantic" art. Thus, he chose a classical theme. Nor was Moreau the only one at this time to turn to the classics for thematic inspiration. There was an exceptional surge of interest in Hellenism in France during the 1850s. Indeed, by 1855, popular admiration for Hellenistic grace and idealism had become a major cultural phenomenon.[25]

The specific inspiration for Moreau's *Athenians* may have been an account which appeared in a current periodical in Moreau's possession. It reported the discovery of the remains of the actual labyrinth at Crete.[26] The subject Moreau chose, however, was drawn from the mythological story in which King Minos of Crete forces Athens to select fourteen youths for sacrifice to the minotaur. Moreau chose to dramatize the confrontation between the Athenians, who represent innocence, and the half-man, half-bull monster who was the tool of King Minos' vengeance in order to emphasize the tension inherent in the mythological episode.

References to a broad spectrum of classical art fill the *Athenians*. For example, the overall composition — with forms created by simplified modeling, strict profiles, compact groupings, and shallow space — suggests a classical frieze, many examples of which were exhibited in the Louvre in Moreau's day. Moreau created the order for his picture by trisecting the composition with the walls of the crumbling labyrinth. He then placed a group of timorous women at the lower left, a more courageous, though equally frightened, group of men in the middle, and the minotaur on the right. The central group, emphasized by the architectural framing and by stronger contrasts of light and dark, he based on David's Neo-Classical masterwork, the *Oath of the Horatii* (fig. 6). In the David painting, the visual grouping reinforces the sense of concerted resolve. Moreau attempts to have his figures suggest the same quality of resolution as they face the approaching monster. From

David, Moreau also borrowed the device of contrasting the stalwart men with the timorous women. On the other hand, the kneeling figure to the right seems to have been taken from Poussin's *Arcadian Shepherds,* also in the Louvre (fig. 7). Like Poussin, Moreau used this figure to point out to his companions the key narrative element in the picture. In Moreau's work it is the minotaur, in Poussin's a tomb inscription.

Moreau's color in the *Athenians* differs markedly from that of his previous work. Despite the fact that his use of bitumen[27] has caused the pigment to disintegrate, enough of the picture remains to reveal its strong and extreme color accents, especially in the cloaks. The contrast between the bright, rich, and varied pigments used for the figures and the dull greenish-grey of the background and foreground is the chief expressive means of this work and suggests the stunning effect of the original painting.

The *Athenians,* Moreau's most important picture to date, was a government commission which paid him four thousand francs,[28] and it was shown in the art exhibition which combined the Salon and the Universal Exhibition of 1855. Although the picture was probably requested as a result of the influence of Moreau's father, its purchase signified that Moreau's work was held in high regard. While both exhibition and purchase must have encouraged him, no critic seems to have noticed the painting. The *Athenians* not only had to compete with a vast number of other entries in the Salon exhibition, which included the large restrospectives of Ingres and Delacroix, but with Courbet's Pavilion of Realism as well.

During the 1850s, Moreau created a number of large paintings which were never completed. He even marked them *"en voie d'exécution"* to indicate that they did not meet his standard of "finish." One of these is *The Daughters of Thestius* (fig 8). The section dating from the 1850s, that is, the dark central portion depicting Hercules sitting among the large group of women to whom he will make love in the course of a single night, demonstrates the same shift from Delacroix and Chasseriau to the new "classical" style seen in the *Athenians*. Moreau's picture is quiet, devoid of the romantic sensuality inherent in the theme. Rather than focusing on Hercules' sexual prowess, Moreau has depicted the hero deep in thought, contemplating his task and perhaps even its significance.

Moreau's shift in style did not mean that he rejected the Old Masters. A fluid and delicate drawing for *Hercules* (cat. no. 14) reveals his continued reliance upon the art of the past. For it, he used sanguine, a red crayon favored by the Old Masters and employed by Moreau only in the 1850s. A specific influence can be detected in *Hercules'* compact pose, which is reminiscent of the contorted nude figures in Michelangelo's Sistine ceiling. In Moreau's picture the compressed pose expresses the physical and emotional stress of Hercules as he anticipates the superhuman activity he is about to undertake.

Moreau followed *Hercules* with *Young Man and Death,* a painting conceived as a memorial to Chasseriau who died in 1856 (although the painting was not finally executed and exhibited until 1865 [fig. 11]). In this work, though he continued to use elements from earlier art, he was forced to develop an original conception as the subject had no clear artistic precedent. In a spirited, rapid preliminary sketch (cat. no. 15), Moreau rejected the idea of a traditional memorial portrait for a more symbolic statement. This painting marked the

I.

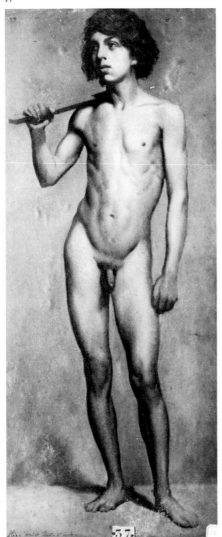

2.

1.
Gustave Moreau
Academie, 1847
Oil on canvas
31½ x 13⅜ in. (80.0 x 34.0 cm.)
Musée Gustave Moreau, Paris

2.
Gustave Boulanger, 1824-1888
*Ulysses Recognized by His Nurse
Eurycleia,* 1849
Oil on canvas
57⁷⁄₁₆ x 44⅛ in. (146.0 x 114.0 cm.)
Ecole des Beaux-Arts, Paris

3.
Gustave Moreau
Sketchbook Page
Pencil on paper
10½ x 6¼ in. (26.6 x 15.9 cm.)
Musée Gustave Moreau, Paris
4.
Gustave Moreau
Study for *Sulamite*
Pencil on paper
7½ x 5½ in. (19.0 x 13.9 cm.)
Musée Gustave Moreau, Paris

5.

5.
Gustave Moreau
Song of Songs, 1853
Oil on canvas
108 x 112 in. (274.4 x 284.6 cm.)
Musée de Dijon

6.

6.
Jacques Louis David, 1748-1825
Oath of the Horatii, 1784
Oil on canvas
130 x 167⅝ in. (330.0 x 425.0 cm.)
Musée du Louvre, Paris
7.
Nicolas Poussin, 1594-1665
The Arcadian Shepherds, 1662
Oil on canvas
33½ x 47⅝ in. (85.1 x 121.0 cm.)
Musée du Louvre, Paris

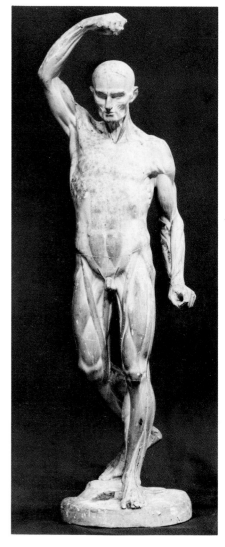

8.
Gustave Moreau
The Daughters of Thestius, ca. 1852-1854
Oil on canvas
101½ x 100⅜ in. (258.0 x 255.0 cm.)
Musée Gustave Moreau, Paris
9.
Cast of Houdon's *Ecorché*
Plaster
H. 19⅞ in. (50.5 cm.)
Musée Gustave Moreau, Paris

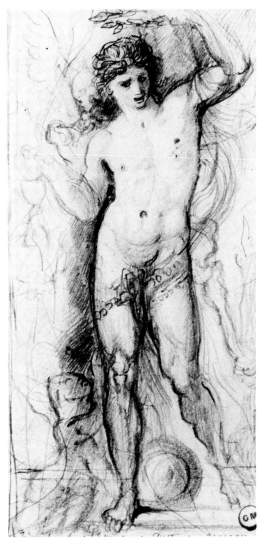

10.
Gustave Moreau
Young Man and Death, ca. 1856
Pencil on paper
9⅛ x 4¼ in. (23.2 x 10.9 cm.)
Musée Gustave Moreau, Paris
11.
Gustave Moreau
Young Man and Death, 1856-65
Oil on canvas
83½ x 48¼ in. (212.2 x 122.6 cm.)
Fogg Art Museum, Harvard University,
Cambridge

12.

12.
Endymion
Carved relief
Capitoline Museum, Rome

beginning of Moreau's involvement with a symbolic method which he pursued throughout his career.

The striding figure in *Young Man and Death* stands for Chasseriau. The identity of the figure behind him is not clear. The young man's pose could have been inspired by any number of antique statues, but Houdon's *Ecorché* is the most likely source since Moreau owned a plaster cast of it (fig. 9). Houdon's image combined a sense of horror, suggested by the flayed body, with the pose used for Greek statues representing victory. He thus brought together the idea of physical mortality and eternal fame, a combination which Moreau used because it effectively expressed Chasseriau's physical death but artistic immortality.

Moreau wrote about this painted homage to Chasseriau in a letter of 1856 to his friend, the painter and writer Eugène Fromentin (1820-1876). By this time he had devised a more detailed idea for the picture (fig. 10) and was contemplating a change which would make the scene more enigmatic. He wrote that he was going to replace the traditional figure of death (which appears as a skeleton in the preliminary drawing) with that of a young woman. He called the putto at the lower left a symbolic and allegorical addition. Moreau's thinking about allegory and symbolism was central to his work. He believed allegory to be a method of using a complex of known symbols to make a definite statement not subject to varied interpretations. In Symbolism, on the other hand, the forms are subject to varied interpretations, for it is a method aimed at suggesting rather than defining. It would seem, then, almost impossible to reconcile allegory and symbolism in a single image, yet this is precisely what Moreau was able to achieve.

This same letter to Fromentin reveals aspects of Moreau's technical method, for instance, his use of photography in place of a live model. He spoke of the freedom with which he sketched his forms once their outlines and interior modeling were set, and added that he hoped his finished work would reveal some of the spontaneity and liveliness of this preparation.[29]

In this period of his career Moreau revealed that the examination of earlier art was a vital ingredient in his attempt to break from the influence of Delacroix and Chasseriau. He must have felt he did not have sufficient knowledge of the art of the past, for he decided to study ancient and Renaissance art by making a trip to Italy.[30]

The Italian trip lasted from November 1857 to August 1859 and took him as far south as Naples. It resulted in friendships with such artists as Degas, the sculptor Henri Chapu (1833-1891), and the academic painter Léon Bonnat (1833-1892) — French artists who were there either as winners of the Prix de Rome or as individual students studying privately. The journey seems to have thoroughly inspired him, for Moreau made hundred of copies in all media (now in the Moreau Museum).

Moreau explored not only ancient art (cat. no. 16) but the whole range of Italian art of the fourteenth and fifteenth centuries. His admiration for the precise linear idiom of what was then thought to be a portrait by Holbein (cat. no. 17) did not preclude an interest in the grandiose drama of Michelangelo (cat. no. 18). As can be seen from a careful and harmonious watercolor after Titian (cat no. 19), he was attracted to Venetian painting with its atmospheric qualities created by fluid strokes of thick oil pigment.

The only original composition of this trip was Moreau's *Hesoid and the Muse* (cat. no. 20).[31] Although this work closely followed the Endymion relief in the Capitoline Museum in Rome (fig. 12), Moreau's adaption was a more "mannered" image. He injected a new note into the classical myth of the Moon, Selene's, love of the youth Endymion. By presenting Endymion as an exhausted adolescent dominated by a female, he suggested a man-woman duality which was to recur frequently in his later work. In Moreau's *Hesoid* anatomical details such as toes and fingers were exaggerated, an unreal geometry was substituted for natural curves (as in the staff the youth holds), profiles were sharpened and distorted, and nudity replaced drapery. But even here, when Moreau was borrowing very closely from a classical source, his approach was clearly a synthetic one, and he freely transformed the mood — if not the imagery — of his source to make a personal statement.

While in Rome Moreau also drew from the model at the French academy in the Villa Medici where the winners of the Prix de Rome lived (cat. nos. 21 and 22).[32] This repetition of academic exercises like those he had done a decade before as a student, signifies that Moreau intended to retrace his footsteps by copying the Old Masters and learning from nature (IV, 17, 19).[33]

At this time also, Moreau turned to landscape studies believing that when an artist could capture the subtleties of nature, he would have mastered color (IV, 113-114). These studies range from crisp views of the Italian coastline, probably done on shipboard while traveling from Rome to Naples (cat. no. 23), to large watercolors and pastels which convey a sense of sunlight and atmosphere (cat. no. 24). Sometimes Moreau would sketch a site so freely that only its color revealed it to be a depiction of a specific moment and place, as for example the dark golden-toned watercolor which suggests autumn (cat. no. 25). Moreau returned to such landscape studies whenever he visited the countryside, as his watercolors and drawings from Etampes and Honfleur in the 1880s testify (cat no. 26).[34]

Although Moreau's studies of nature never became a key focus of his art, his examination of it was one of his means of moving toward a personal style. He was interested in all aspects of day and night — morning mist or evening fog. At certain rare moments he even approached genre when he was especially struck by something he had seen, for instance a peasant observed from the back and recorded as a memoir of his Italian trip (cat. no. 27). Nor was Moreau completely immune to the forces motivating the contemporary movements of Realism and Naturalism. Indeed, the evidence of his interest in and talent for realistic subject matter makes it all the more clear that his decision not to pursue these aesthetic tendencies, but rather to develop a more imaginative synthesis of his own, was made deliberately and not by default.

The 1860s

By the 1860s Moreau was recognized as one of the most noted painters in France. As a result of his careful study in Italy, his paintings eventually achieved an unmistakably personal stamp; becoming fully developed statements of an ideal-sensual dualism; making extensive use of literary and artistic sources; and employing a distinctive allegorical and symbolic method. It had taken several years for Moreau to assimilate the lessons learned in Italy sufficiently to be able to produce and exhibit a large finished painting. The pictures in his *Stations of the Cross* at Nôtre Dame, Decazeville are the only major works from the early sixties, but apparently even they did not satisfy Moreau for he wished them to remain anonymous.[35]

As early as 1861 Moreau began slowly and carefully preparing for his re-entry into the artistic spotlight of the Paris Salon with *Oedipus and the Sphinx*[36] (cat. nos. 28 and 29). Indeed, when this painting was exhibited in the Salon of 1864, it created such a sensation that Daumier and other popular caricaturists of the day reproduced it for the popular press[37] (fig. 13). The subject of the painting derives, of course, from classical literature. It deals with the young Theban hero, Oedipus, who liberates his city from the tyranny of the monstrous sphinx by answering its famous riddle. Thereafter, he unwittingly kills his father, the King of Thebes, and marries his mother, the Queen. Discovering what he has done, he blinds himself and ends his days wandering the face of the earth. From the many possibilities offered by this monstrous and chilling tale, Moreau chose to depict the moment Oedipus solves the sphinx's riddle. He presents a confident Oedipus looking straight ahead, as though through the sphinx, who in turn is wide-eyed and open mouthed as if shocked that Oedipus has succeeded where all before him failed. Although both figures are still and quiet, violence is implied by the fact that the sphinx has sprung upon Oedipus' body.

Obviously the picture is not merely an illustration of a scene from ancient literature but is intended to convey several ideas that preoccupied Moreau.[38] The imagery Moreau selected and the specific symbols he employed suggest that the picture is concerned with confrontations between the forces of life and death, male principle and female, and, finally, good and evil. In a note[39] he explained that the picture represented man facing the eternal mystery and that, although this mystery is both dangerous and tempting, man's moral strength makes him confront it with self-confidence (III, 21). Because Moreau was aware of the traditional association of the sphinx with voluptuousness, he conceived *Oedipus and the Sphinx* in terms of a conflict between moral idealism and sensual desire.

Moreau saw this same conflict embodied in the Italian Quattrocento painting he had been studying.[40] The sad, mysterious, and meditative faces of the figures animating this art communicated to him a sense of both the physical and spiritual nature of man, of the merging of the real and the ideal which represented the union between man and God. Because these pictures stimulated a sense of knowing that transcended the limits of his rational faculties, Moreau called them "divine." Indeed, he thought it miraculous that looking at Quattrocento painting could inspire such "thoughts." Because this earlier art dealt so effectively with the very same problems which interested him and which continued to be relevant in his own time — that is, the dualism of body and spirit — he decided to employ a related and equally "sacred" style.

If Moreau was influenced by fifteenth-century Italian painting while creating the *Oedipus,* other influences were at work on him as well. He looked to Ingres, for example, when he was developing his first ideas for the painting (cat. no. 30). The inclusion of these early sketches in a book dedicated to ancient statues he had seen in Rome,[41] however, suggests that *Oedipus* was more than just a variant on Ingres' conception of this theme; rather Moreau wanted his scene to be as full of expressive power as the greatly revered monuments from antiquity. To achieve this general end, as well as the more specific objective of creating a static depiction of a direct physical confrontation, he supplemented Ingres' prototypes with classical and Persian scenes of confrontations between man and beast, i.e. *Hercules and the Nemean Lion* and a winged lion fighting a hero (figs. 14 and 15). The Persian image bears a thematic as well as a structural resemblance to the *Oedipus,* for it too represents the idea of good versus evil.[42]

While Oedipus' pose could have come from any number of antique or Renaissance sources, most contemporary critics thought Mantegna supplied the model. For a picture such as *St. Sebastian* (Louvre), for example, this assertion is most likely correct, but a more important point than the exact source is the general fact that Moreau was still relying heavily on the art of the past to create his image.

The mysteriousness at the core of *Oedipus and the Sphinx* derives from a characteristic he borrowed from Michelangelo and employed for the first time in this work: the use of static figures whose staring expressions suggest they are lost in thought or dream. Moreau himself said that his pictures were mysterious (III, 50) and one reason for this was the characteristic transfixed quality of the figures in them. He called this stasis *"la belle inertie."*[43] He wrote that all the figures in Michelangelo's work seemed to be asleep —their movements unconscious. They seem absorbed in a dream world and inhabit a divine and non-material realm quite different from our own. They do not enact clearly recognizable scenes, and in some inexplicable way their actual movements often seem in contradiction to the meaning we attach to them. Despite our curiosity, they are enigmatic and puzzling and refuse to let us know what they are doing and thinking.[44]

Apparently Moreau was enthralled with the sense of mystery communicated by Michelangelo's work and considered the effect excellently suited to painting. He decided to use it in *Oedipus* where he created static composition which nonetheless suggests elemental and continuous strife. It is precisely the "illogic" of the statement, the contradiction implicit in it, that insures its powerful evocativeness and frees it from the limitations of imagery too readily comprehended. For, although both the Sphinx and Oedipus have fixed, controlled, and even somewhat vacant facial expressions, the posture of the sphinx, upon Oedipus, implies a violent action. This contradiction makes the image suggestive beyond the allegorical level on which the specific symbols are totally comprehensible and therefore able to move the spectator emotionally. Thus, Moreau solved the problem of creating a statement that is on one level comprehensible and yet on another remains sufficiently mysterious and incomprehensible to be evocative as well.

Though it is Michelangelo's art that underlies Moreau's basic approach in *Oedipus,* the linear style of the work is reminiscent of a quite different artist, Carpaccio, in whose *St. George* the dramatic confrontation between man and beast is represented in the same frozen manner. Moreau had copied this painting in a huge canvas, now in the Moreau Museum (No. 195).

To neither Michelangelo nor Carpaccio can the synthesis arrived at in the *Oedipus* be attributed. Rather, it was Poussin who became Moreau's most fundamental model in this regard. Though Moreau did not borrow specifics from Poussin's paintings, he found in them a precedent for an art based on a precise linear technique, yet able to achieve a free and imaginative effect, and, still more importantly, a precedent for a synthesizing method which picks and chooses from the whole history of art. He praised Poussin as an academic artist but still more as an imaginative producer of evocative work (III, 3-4).

Moreau's earliest dated idea for the *Oedipus* theme is a drawing of 1860 whose composition is repeated in a watercolor (cat. no. 31). The scene is active and dramatic, reminiscent of his earlier style. By 1861, however, Moreau had decided to employ a poised and static composition to create a more symbolic and thus more evocative image of struggle. A precedent for this change in Moreau's approach had already been intimated in the *Athenians* in 1855, but it only became an explicit stylistic trait in the 1860s.

Though the idea for *Oedipus* had been developed by 1861, the picture was not exhibited until 1864. The long delay between conception and conclusion resulted from Moreau's belief — acquired at the Ecole des Beaux-Arts — that a picture must be prepared with numerous studies. His notes record the process. First, he drew from the live model; next, he used little figurines to reveal how the shadows would fall over figures and setting; and then he used both living model and small clay figures to study the drapery. Once such pictorial problems had been solved to Moreau's satisfaction, he enlarged his composition and/or transferred it to another canvas or piece of paper until he arrived at the final size of the picture. The most common method used to achieve this change in size was squaring (cat. no. 32), and Moreau's use of this method reveals an indifference to scale, not unusual for his time. An image that might be totally satisfactory when it was small, when enlarged might look quite different. A fresh and sensitive view from nature (cat. no. 32) contrasts markedly in style with a hard and stiff detail for the painting (cat. no. 33). Yet, this method was the one prescribed by tradition. Indeed, it was the one used by the majority of figure painters at this time — and it accounts for the lack of coherence and spontaneity in much of their art. So codified was technique that the only time an academic artist thought deeply about his picture was in conceiving it. The execution was a mechanical process that almost took care of itself. The academic style of *Oedipus* is found throughout Moreau's work in the 1860s. Precise draftsmanship characterizes the contours; modeling results from miniscule hatching strokes; and large figures dominate settings — often barren — which are illuminated by an unnatural light.

The *Oedipus,* then, is both evocative (symbolic) and allegorical, since Moreau assigned specific meanings to his symbols. Visually, the two main figures carry the symbolic weight of the picture. Writing to Fromentin in 1856 about

Young Man and Death (fig. 11) and *Jason and Medea* (fig. 16), Moreau stated that the interpretation of the painting would vary with each viewer. However, he also said that for him the picture had a specific meaning and exact symbols. First of all, he considered the sphinx to be very dangerous, and to illustrate the perilousness of attempting to struggle with this monster he placed in the foreground the hand and foot of what appears to be a previous victim. These anatomical details, taken from Ingres' painting of the same subject, reinforce the idea of the fatality of the physical conflict. Moreau makes Oedipus' victory a moral achievement by showing a snake coiling around a column to the lower right and a butterfly hovering above it. He makes the accomplishment a poetic victory by adding a laurel plant. The traditional symbolism of the snake is death, and that of the butterfly the soul. The butterfly's escape from the snake is a symbol of Oedipus' victory, an idea restated by the laurel plant, used in antiquity to crown heroes and poets. The occurrence of an ornamental pedestal, which also follows a classical tradition (similar pedestals are depicted in scenes appearing on ancient gems), underscores the visionary aspect of the picture, but it also could have had a phallic significance which Moreau, living in a pre-Freudian age may or may not have been conscious of. Nonetheless, it reinforces the dichotomy between male and female inherent in the picture by suggesting the idea of masculine potency, domination, and pride.

Moreau's writings, as recorded in the Moreau Museum notebooks, supports the contention that *Oedipus* may have had specific autobiographical significance. The battle of Oedipus with the Sphinx may be related to the personal dilemma Moreau faced in choosing to dedicate himself to an artistic vocation at the expense of sensual gratification. His career can be equated with the ideal, his sacrifice with the real or sensual. In his notes he discusses his art and ideas in a manner reminiscent of his discussion of *Oedipus*. For instance, he contrasts what he calls his own ideal dreams with the temptations and sensuality of the art then fashionable (III, 120-124). He wrote that he felt disgust and hatred for the low, greedy, sensual, and materialistic spirit of his civilization (III, 118); that in his day false and ephemeral works were considered by imbecilic critics and the public to be truly original, while healthy, intelligent, noble, and traditional works were called old fashioned. He accused his contemporaries of confusing eroticism or earthly passion with artistic and creative passion in which the spirit struggles to rise above sensuality (III, 120). The bitter tone of these comments stem from the fact that Moreau's work was often unfavorably criticized in the press. He was perhaps excessively sensitive to such criticism while ignoring the remarks of those critics who reacted favorably to his work.

Although Moreau's aesthetic theory, based upon a belief in the fundamental antagonism of the sensual and the ideal, follows traditional Neo-Platonic philosophy, his position is not exclusively intellectual. In Moreau's case the theory may have been an outgrowth of his feelings about physical passion. Both the *Oedipus* and Moreau's writings about it reveal that Moreau was simultaneously opposed to and fascinated by sensuality. He once wrote that ideal communion with the Divine was a "refound virginity" (III, 93-94), a phrase which is interesting for its equation of the ideal and the non-sexual.

Moreau's symbolic method can be investigated further in the two major works he produced immediately following the *Oedipus,* the two large pictures he showed in the Salon of 1865, *Young Man and Death* (cat. no. 15) and *Jason and Medea* (fig. 16).45 In the former the young man emerges from a wooded garden holding a laurel wreath over his head. Since the laurel is a traditional symbol of artistic merit, his gesture can be interpreted as one of self-glorification. The figure's youthfulness and action of rewarding his own genius are in contrast to the finitude of human mortality, symbolized by the freshly cut flowers the boy holds which will soon wither and die; by the smoldering torch held by the putto below, which will soon go out; and even perhaps by the bird to the right, which is in the process of flying away. Death is personified by a somnolent young woman who holds the attributes of mortality, a sword and an hourglass. Traditionally Death is depicted as a man. By personifying Death as a young woman, Moreau may have been giving further expression to a negative and fatal view of woman, implicit in the female Sphinx figure he had used in *Oedipus.*

The symbolic values assigned to the figures in *Young Man and Death* are strengthened by Moreau's careful manipulation of significant details. For example, he gives the young man a convincing physical reality by making his posture very definite and by positioning his feet firmly on the ground. The brightness of the light falling on him models his form into a convincing, solid presence and distinguishes him from the rest of the scene. In contrast, the young woman, seated behind him to indicate her secondary position, is less imbued with vitality. There is no visible means of support for her body, and her drapery seems to be blown upward by some invisible, yet powerful draft. All of these elements add a certain mysteriousness and intangibility to the figure, endow her, in fact, with a sense of the supernatural. By making the figure representing Chasseriau so much stronger than that of Death, Moreau was able to express the idea that Chasseriau's art triumphs over his physical demise.

Because *Young Man and Death* was conceived in the 1850s but executed in the 1860s, it is useful as an example of Moreau's aesthetic evolution in the later decade — his increasing concern with allegory and symbolism, and, in terms of technique, his growing reliance on a linear style. Although on an allegorical level the painting has the specific meaning discussed above, its symbolism also functions on other, less specific, but more suggestive levels. These include, for instance, the figures' frozen postures, the inexplicable force responsible for lifting the young woman's drapery, and the young man's drapery which so perfectly fits his genitals and thereby evokes a sense of his potency. Thus, the function of the imagery has been expanded so that it not only illustrates specific points but opens up a host of possible interpretations. Such defiance of precise definition is a salient aspect of Moreau's mature style and can be seen again in two pencil sketches (cat. nos. 34 and 35) of his next major work, *Jason and Medea.*

Like *Oedipus* and *Young Man, Jason and Medea* depicts a moment of victory. In the myth of Jason and the golden fleece, Cupid forces Medea to fall in love with Jason and to use her magic to help him even though it causes the deaths of her father and brother. When Jason eventually deserts Medea for another woman, she seeks to revenge herself by killing their two children as well as his new fiancée.

The painting of *Jason and Medea* (fig. 16) provides the only example in all of Moreau's oeuvre of a direct literary quotation. On the column at the left side of the picture Moreau inscribed two quotations from Ovid, which he used as the basis for his imagery. One of the quotations refers to Medea's overpowering love of and devotion to Jason.[46] The other passage reveals her responsibility for his victory.[47] Moreau took liberties with his literary source, however, depicting Jason as the hero responsible for killing the monster that guards the fleece rather than following Ovid's example and making Medea charm the monster to sleep.

Visually, the two figures, in both the drawings and the painting (cat. nos. 34, 35, and fig. 16), relate to each other in a manner at once calm and subtle. Their compositional placement, postures, and the direction of their gazes are vital in communicating the meaning of the picture. In the first drawing and in the painting the two figures overlap in such a way that their contours combine to form one large configuration. In the first drawing also (cat. no. 34) Medea has her arm around Jason's chest and is looking at him as he holds the fleece. Moreau dramatizes Medea's not only powerful but dominant role by making her taller than Jason, by placing her in the exact center of the composition clasping him, and by directing her gaze at him. In the second drawing (cat. no. 35), a study for Jason's pose, Jason appears alone and seems to be looking at his hand. His stance in this instance suggests that he, too, plays a major part in the victory.

In the final painting (fig. 16) once again Jason and Medea's positions indicate that Medea is the more powerful figure and more responsible for the victory. Her strength is reinforced by such supernatural symbols as the snake she holds and the sphinx which, significantly, caps the "phallic" victory column — a symbol of Jason — and thereby indicates her ascendency over him. But Jason's strength is dramatized too as he is depicted bearing the broken spear with which he has killed the monster.

A respect in which the painting differs from the two preliminary drawings is the presence of a long pole-like form separating the two figures, rising above their heads and ending below Jason's heel. It carries a caduceus surmounted by a gold and blue ball, probably the one Aphrodite promised Cupid if he would make Medea fall in love with Jason.[48] This magic wand was the chief attribute of Mercury, the messenger of the gods, and its presence in the scene symbolizes the intervention of the gods and their participation in the victory. The fact that the wand stands between the couple also forebodes the eventual doom that will befall their relationship.

Jason and Medea parallels Moreau's previous paintings of the 1860s. All are large and vertical in format and are based on classical mythology. All represent scenes dominated by large figures, often occurring in barren mountainous settings which include elaborate decorative columns. The adolescent androgynous types Moreau used repeatedly are based upon the young Italian models he studied in Picot's studio and the figures he copied from Italian Quattrocento masters such as Uccello and Verocchio. Moreau's own stature was small and delicate, and this too may have contributed to his choice of this physical type. However, the sensitive and delicate drawing (cat. no. 36) for the figure of Jason is precise enough to indicate that Moreau hired a specific model for the Jason figure.[49]

Because Delacroix had done a painting of the same subject (fig. 17), Moreau's work has the added interest of revealing his growing emancipation from Delacroix's influence. In fact, it is possible that Moreau may have been attracted to the subject of Medea precisely because it provided a means for him to express his independence of Delacroix. However, what probably prompted his picture was the play *Medée* which had been written by his friend Ernest Legouvé in 1854. A copy of the play was in Moreau's library, and he may well have seen it performed. Since in this play Medea is portrayed as innocent and betrayed, obviously it was no more than a point of departure for Moreau. It may have stimulated him to reread Ovid and then develop his own version of the story with its moralizing statement.[50]

The moment Moreau chose to depict was one in which Jason and Medea appear to be cooperating, and male and female forces to be equal. Moreau counterbalances the strength of one sex with that of the other, but he also suggests visually that the stable relationship will be impermanent. The cause of the instability is considered in one of Moreau's notes (III, 19) in which he wrote of Jason's egomania and his disregard for Medea's love. It is his selfishness and her excessive devotion that produce the tragedy that ultimately befalls this pair. Nor did Moreau believe the evil effect of these passions to be limited to Jason and Medea. He felt that arrogance and romantic obsession have plagued mankind throughout the ages.

In the *Orpheus* (cat. no. 38), Moreau's entry for the Salon of 1866, he returned to the theme of spirit versus matter or sensuality using Orpheus to symbolize art and the frenzied Bacchantes to represent uncontrolled passion. (The Salon picture was purchased by the government and is now in the Louvre. Cat. no. 38 is a reduced replica.) In the traditional legend, Orpheus, the greatest of all musicians, was symbolic of the artist and, by extension, of civilization. He was torn apart by a group of women at a Dionysiac orgy and the parts of his body were cast into the river Hebros. The moment Moreau chose is one which occurs in the aftermath of this tragedy. In the Salon catalog Moreau added the following sentence after the title: "A young girl piously gathers up Orpheus' head and his lyre, brought by the Hebros to the shores of Thrace."[51] He depicts a young girl from Thrace weeping as she mourns the lyre and head she has retrieved from the river. The necrophilic possibilities of the myth are reduced to a minimum, and the picture is strangely quiet and restful. It is quite the antipode of the *Diomedus Eaten by His Horses* (Musée de Rouen) which Moreau also entered in the same Salon of 1866 and which represented his only return to the aggresive violence of his earlier work.

The general mood of *Orpheus* is sympathetic and the work is a relatively gentle, straightforward statement of the tragedy faced by the creative individual. In the background of the picture a shepherd pipes the music that Orpheus gave to mankind, and in the foreground are two turtles, symbolic of the domestic virtues of the young woman.[52] The most important figure in the composition is the young woman, and moreover, she is the only person with a specific symbolic attribute. In fact, this is the first time Moreau has made a positive statement about a woman in any of his works.

The drawing for *Orpheus* (cat. no. 39) represents that stage in Moreau's preparation of the picture after the idea had been conceived and sketched. The hard contours indicate final compositional decisions which were later transferred to the canvas in the finished painting. *End.*

The watercolor *The Saint and the Poet* (cat. no. 40) (Salon of 1869) epitomizes the linear style Moreau developed in the 1860s and has the precision of manuscript illumination. The watercolor, which treats the story of Saint Elizabeth of Hungary, suggests that religious miracle is the basis for artistic inspiration, and introduces for the first time in Moreau's oeuvre an association of art and religion. In this work Moreau followed the legend of this saint's life, which includes an incident when roses appeared miraculously out-of-season. Moreau has the miracle occur just as a poet bows in adoration before the image of the saint. Although he used watercolor in this instance, Moreau apparently had no particular interest in the fluid effects that could be produced with this medium and did not exploit it to that end. Rather, he used it to create a precise image just as if he were drawing or painting.

The *Prometheus* of 1868 (cat. no. 41) was another of his pictures to be included in the Salon of 1869. Its theme was a very popular one in the nineteenth century when poets and artists alike were attracted to the figure of the archetypal hero who stole fire from the gods to give to mankind and who in consequence suffered the torment of having his liver eternally eaten by a vulture. The theme attracted Moreau, too, and he followed the nineteenth-century literary tradition that saw the lonely, tormented, and self-sacrificing Prometheus as a symbol of Christ and/or the creative artist.[53] Moreau wrote that he wanted to show a man of thought attacked by the torments and brutality of matter but at the same time resigned to his fate and confident of the future (II, 73). Basically, *Prometheus,* like *Oedipus,* is a symbolic representation of Moreau's philosophic belief that man has sufficient moral strength and intellectual idealism to combat the sensuousness of his own nature.

In *Prometheus* Moreau repeated what by now had become a compositional formula for him: the placement of a static figure in a barren, mountainous setting which includes an ornamental column. In this instance the landscape setting, which represents a mythical site in the Caucasus, is dominated by Prometheus who is placed slightly off-center and to the left, poised above a deep chasm. The major impact of the picture results from the figure's tense immobility. His face is mask-like with its stern profile, generalized features, wig-like hair, and straight beard corresponding to and repeating the shape of his forehead. Prometheus' tension is expressed by the jutting contours of his body, his flexed limbs and the tautness of his neck and forearm. Moreau experimented with fifteen variants in over sixty drawings to arrive at the final image.

It is Prometheus' tension and the tight compression of his posture that produce the impression of strength and make believable the self-control that allows him to endure the pain the vulture causes him. It is his expression — he stares impassively into the distance — that implies a sense of confidence and the ability to endure his fate. The body of the vulture below him, apparently dead, suggests that his torture may be about to end. Undoubtedly Moreau identified with Prometheus' suffering, seeing in it an analogue of his own artistic struggle, and he may also have identified, albeit subconsciously, with the powerful masculinity of this mythical figure. Certainly, the virility of Prometheus' figure is pronounced. Not only his pose, but the drapery which exposes

and defines his genitals, communicate his maleness which is also underlined by the ornamental column with its phallic associations. In sum, the figure is a powerful, masculine one that serves simultaneously as a projection of Moreau's self-conception and as a symbol to express the very concept of idealism.

For *Prometheus* Moreau once again synthesized a large variety of past art. The landscape background, for instance, is reminiscent of the type seen in the paintings of Leonardo. The figure of Prometheus, on the other hand, is based on a nude male figure — in a similar pose and often shown with an ornamental pedestal — that appears frequently on antique engraved gems (fig. 18); the figure is that of Marsyas, the satyr flayed by Apollo for daring to challenge him. Like Prometheus, Marsyas can be considered a type of martyr, which would account for Moreau's attraction to this source. One of Moreau's drawings (fig. 19) reveals that he had also thought of borrowing from Jean-Jacques Pradier's Prometheus statue (fig. 20) in the Tuileries Gardens. In Pradier's statue a dead bird appears below Prometheus, just as it does in Moreau's painting.

Moreau's attraction to the Prometheus legend is one more instance of his devotion to mythology, a devotion he shared with an author whose writing he found very enlightening, Louis Ménard. In his writing Ménard expressed the belief that mythology stemmed from actual events which occurred in ancient times. Moreau, too, believed this, as well as the fact that mythological themes had particular power because they presented problems which had persisted from antiquity to his own day (III, 118) and thus were statements at once intensely personal, contemporary, and universal, as he wished his own work to be.

Ménard's poem "Prometheus Delivered" appears to have been the model for the imagery in Moreau's *Prometheus:*
Les astres d'or roulant aux éternelles sphères
Achèvent lentement leur cours silencieux;
L'encens et la rumeur des plaintives prières
Ont cessé de monter vers le tyran des cieux
Je veille seul: il n'est pour moi ni nuit ni rêve
Et l'immortel vautour ne laisse pas de trêve
A mes flancs déchirés que nourrit la douleur;
Depuis quatre mille ans sa rage me dévore,
Mais les temps vont enfin s'accomplir, et l'aurore
Doit éclairer les pas de mon libérateur.[54]

In Moreau's painting, as in this poem, the time of day is approaching dawn when the sky is beginning to change color in the distance. Prometheus' alertness, the tension of his pose, and his staring eyes suggest that the night has been a sleepless, dreamless one for him. Although aspects of Moreau's image — the vulture's bloody beak and Prometheus' wound — graphically illustrate Prometheus' torture, the fact that the mythic hero is concentrating so fixedly on the distance reveals his anticipation of the arrival of his liberator, Hercules, who was to come the next day.

Ménard's poem also hints at Prometheus' great pride which Moreau manages to suggest by his facial expression and stance. Ménard's dead vulture falling in the distance is placed by Moreau at Prometheus' feet.

All in all, Moreau was strongly influenced by Ménard's poem, and especially by those ideas that conformed to his own

22207

1388. OEDIPE ET LE SPHINX, par GUSTAVE MOREAU.

— Dis donc... c'est pas une bête... c'est h'un Moreau... je viens d'entendre dire à un civil : « *Tenez, voilà l' Moreau.* »

— Ah ! oui... mais quoi que c'est-t'i' qu'un Moreau ?

— Ah ! ben... vas-y demander !

14.   15.

13.
A. Grevin
Caricature from *Le Journal Amusant,*
Paris, 1864, No. 439
Musée Gustave Moreau, Paris
◀

14.
Gustave Moreau
Copy of *Hercules and the Nemean Lion*
Pencil on paper
10⅜ x 7⅞ in. (26.4 x 20.0 cm.)
Musée Gustave Moreau, Paris
15.
Gustave Moreau
Copy of an Assyrian relief from the
Magasin Pittoresque, 1834, p. 343
Pen and ink on tracing paper
4¾ x 3½ in. (12.1 x 8.9 cm.)
Musée Gustave Moreau, Paris

16.

17.

16.
Gustave Moreau
Jason and Medea, 1865
Oil on canvas
80 x 45 in. (203.3 x 114.3 cm.)
Musée du Louvre, Paris

17.
Eugene Delacroix, 1798-1863
Medea, 1862
Oil on canvas
103 x 65 in. (260.0 x 165.0 cm.)
Musée de Lille

18.
Plaster cast of Apollo and Marsyas
from *Collection de Medailles Anciennes
et Pierres Gravées au Palais du Vatican et
dans le Divers Musées de Rome,* Paris,
1859
Musée Gustave Moreau, Paris

19.
Gustave Moreau
Study for *Prometheus,* after Pradier
Pencil on paper
6¾ x 4⁵⁄₁₆ in. (17.2 x 11.0 cm.)
Musée Gustave Moreau, Paris

20.

20.
Jean-Jacques Pradier, 1792-1852
Prometheus, 1827
Marble
H. 73½ in. (186.7 cm.)
Tuileries Gardens, Paris

philosophy, for example the belief that one should suffer stoically.

Increasingly during this decade of the sixties Moreau's pictures came to be the butt of negative criticism in reviews of the Salons. By 1869 a large body of critical opinion had accused him of faulty drawing and a weak sense of color.[55] Even Gautier, a critic generally favorably disposed toward Moreau's work, stated that what had seemed new and striking in 1864, with *Oedipus*, no longer excited the public in 1869.[56] In response to the waning of interest in his art and the criticism of his technique, Moreau stopped exhibiting and began to search out technical changes.

Some of the results of his search are visible in *Prometheus*, which he never sold and which differs technically from Moreau's paintings discussed thus far. Though the carefully defined figure of Prometheus and the form of the vulture are characterized by the same small, laborious hatching strokes that were typical of Moreau's style throughout the sixties, the strong outline around Prometheus' legs, the highlights established with a single stroke, and the thicker impasto are all part of a new "painterly" style. So, too, are the sparkling touches of light, the intense blues in the sky, and the broad, energetic, loaded strokes of the palette knife which describe the drapery. These are Moreau's later additions, and in a note written in December 1882 he mentions wishing to rework pictures like the *Athenians, Song of Songs* (he called it *Sulamite*), and his *Pietà*. He notes, too, that he has already begun repainting *Darius* (see footnote 23), now in the Moreau Museum (No. 223), in which heavy, dark outlines have been superimposed over the more academically modeled figures. The hues, too, are more intense in certain areas than in others — also a characteristic of Prometheus and a reflection of the new stylistic direction Moreau was pursuing.

Despite the fact that there were some critics who consistently admired Moreau's art, he focused only on the negative criticism of his work and, therefore, refused to exhibit between 1869 and 1876. It would seem that he agreed with the main thrust of this negative criticism and himself felt some need to develop a new style. But the philosophical basis of his art and his allegorical-symbolic method he never seriously questioned despite the fact that these, too, were criticized.

From the very beginning of his artistic career, his Idealist philosophy had awakened lively reactions, from the greatest praise[57] to the most profound disdain.[58] Moreau must have realized that these reactions depended totally on the ideologies of the critics. For example, critics like Champfleury, who favored the Realism and Naturalism of Courbet and Manet, considered Moreau's work old fashioned and uninspired. But, other critics, such as Maxime du Camp, more hospitable to academic and Romantic art and believing man's spiritual life to be the proper subject matter for art were highly responsive to Moreau's work and saw in it a unique and rich representation of man's idealism and spirituality.

Any overview of Moreau's work of the 1860s must isolate as particularly significant his synthesizing approach. Based upon antique and Renaissance visual prototypes and classical and contemporary literary sources, he developed a restrained, personal imagery. His literary sources were extremely varied — from Ovid, to Louis Ménard. His models from the visual arts ranged from antique gems, to standard studio props (Houdon's *Ecorché*), to French academic sculpture (Pradier), to painters as diverse as Michelangelo and Poussin. His borrowings from literary and pictorial prototypes were more frequent at this time — the formative phase of his career — than ever again in his artistic development though he never waivered from this basic synthesizing approach. Even at the end of his life he told his students that to be modern does not mean to ignore past achievements, but rather to conserve the discoveries of preceding ages so that this knowledge can be used in the present.[59] He also told them not to fear the Old Masters but to use them as a means of finding a personal direction.[60] Moreau himself never thought his borrowings made his art any less original. Although he tended to base his images on existing sources, he always expressed them in his own formal language. Moreau's extensive use of sources was, in fact, a practice he shared with the art of his age. Even an artist as revolutionary as Manet relied extensively upon earlier art.[61]

As for Moreau's philosophical position, this, too, can be understood more readily in the context of the ideas current in France during the nineteenth century. During Moreau's formative years, Neo-Platonic Idealism was the ascendant philosophical fashion. A book in Moreau's library by Charles Blanc, published in 1867,[62] and Madame de Stael's metaphysical aesthetics, could have influenced him as could the eclecticism of Victor Cousin (1792-1867), an Idealist philosopher whose followers dominated the realm of French philosophy (although at this time Auguste Comte's Positivism was beginning to gain popularity). It was the Neo-Platonism of Jouffroy, however, that most clearly provided Moreau with a philosophical basis for his art. The fact that Jouffroy's lectures of 1822 were published in 1843, when Moreau was at the impressionable age of eighteen, creates the suspicion that Moreau's own philosophical theory was merely a paraphrase of them. Jouffroy said that appearances — phenomena as we see them — are only a mask hiding a greater reality; that Beauty — a symbolic disclosure of the invisible — stirs our souls with its suggestiveness, and that in a truly aesthetic culture the spirit is led to the light of Beauty which only men of genius and insight are able to grasp.[63] No doubt Jouffroy's system appealed to Moreau because of his predilection for the eternal aspects of life and his contempt for the then current fashion of eroticism and materialism.

Moreau's own writings are in a sense Neo-Platonic as they are based on his belief that the passions should be elevated, refined, and given an abstract expression.[64] He wrote that the artist should employ stoic restraint to repudiate his earthly sensibilities and ultimately achieve the realm of divine feeling where he can produce a universal statement capable of ennobling and transfiguring the human soul. Moreau saw this transfiguration as part of an enigmatic process in which "divine joy" is converted into the creative energy that produces art. He believed that as human beings we have intuitions — God-given insights arising unconsciously — which allow us to transcend what we can merely perceive and to experience sublime elation. To Moreau this transcendental insight was the only reliable basis for art, and his aesthetic theory is based on this belief in what he called "inner enlightenment."

It was the need to find a method of translating his philosophical beliefs into a painter's technique that led Moreau to evolve his particular kind of symbolic-allegorical approach (an approach not fully consistent with that of the late nineteenth-century Symbolists, who also attempted to translate ideas about "intuition" and "evocation" into a system of painting.) As we have seen, Moreau's method was dependent on the existence, on different symbolic levels, of a single set of specific pictorial facts. These "facts" occur on the level of simple allegory as well as on a more abstract symbolic level where the pictorial elements are evocative and suggestive in a more open-ended manner. It is this aspect of his art that makes him one of the precursors of Symbolism.

The particular thematic content of his images link Moreau to Romanticism. In *Oedipus and the Sphinx* and *Young Man and Death* the theme is the conflict and suffering which results when man's idealism and physical desires are pitted against each other; in *Jason and Medea* the theme is one of romantic disillusionment; in *Prometheus* and *Orpheus* it is the isolation and torment of the artist. All are basic in the Romantic declaration of faith.[65]

Moreau's Romanticism was stylistically eclectic. Not just in the 1860s, but throughout his artistic career, he retained a flexibility of stance which permitted him to borrow from all available sources and artistic methods.

Moreau's work of the 1870s and 1880s was profoundly affected by the stylistic investigations he had been engaged in during the six years he refrained from public exhibition. To refute the criticism he had received in the 1860s, he spent the years from 1870 through 1875 exploring new technical possibilities and alternative subject matter and seeking inspiration from fresh visual sources. The results of his study are embodied in *Salome Dancing before Herod* (cat. no. 42) and *Hercules and the Hydra of Lerna* (cat. no. 50) (Salon of 1876).

Salome Dancing before Herod is based on the well-known Biblical story of the young princess who danced before her stepfather to win the head of John the Baptist for her mother, Herodias. Moreau's interest in the subject stemmed from his belief that he could use it to make a strong statement about women. For, to Moreau, Salome was an extremely forceful figure, a woman at once mysterious and fatal, "a woman in search of a vague, sensual, and unhealthy ideal, who destroys men, be they geniuses or saints" (III, 49). Moreau went to great pains to create an image of Salome which would do justice to his conception of her. To achieve an aura of mystery, he felt it necessary that her dance of the seven veils be an evocative (symbolic) image, explaining that he wanted Salome to be a sibyl possessing the ancient psychic power of the seer. Because he also wanted to utilize the power inherent in religious imagery, he decided to make her a sacred enchantress as well.[66] He wished to depict her as a kind of reliquary, a holy ceremonial object.[67] Moreau probably chose this image for two reasons: first, because it was rich in symbolic associations whose mystery he wanted Salome to possess, and, second, because the form of a reliquary — architectonic, rigid, and richly decorated — offered him a new stylistic direction to follow for his conception of the picture.

Because sensual temptation was a prevalent theme in Moreau's art during the sixties, Salome, as one of the best known examples of a temptress, was an apt subject. Moreover, because of her Biblical association, he could use her to state his ideas about the fatality of woman and still be able to infuse that statement with the transcendental power of religious art. Simultaneously, he could display his knowledge of the Orient, gleaned from extensive reading. The idea of combining the fatal woman, religious faith, and the Orient seems to have derived from Moreau's favorite French author, Chateaubriand, whom he admired greatly for his deep sense of disenchantment, the desperation of his dreams, his idealism, and his sincere religious faith.[68] This combination of elements was in perfect accord with Moreau's art theory.

It seems likely that Moreau connected the idea of Salome as a fatal woman with his interest in Eastern art not only because of Chateaubriand but because the literature of Moreau's time provided a roster of destructive and beautiful oriental women who could be used as prototypes for Salome. There were for instance, Gautier's *Une Nuit de Cléopâtre* (1838), Flaubert's *Salammbô* (1862),[69] as well as Mallarmé's *Hérodias* (1871).[70] French painting at this time, too, was flooded with oriental themes. The specific impetus for Moreau's work may have been a painting by an artist he greatly admired, Henri Regnault, whose *Salome* had won a prize in the Salon of 1869 (fig. 21), the very Salon in which Moreau's works had been criticized. It is certainly conceivable that the subject which won praise at the moment that his own work was found lacking assumed a special prominence in his thoughts.

Moreau scoured the history of art for visual ideas he could use in *Salome*. Especially struck by the elaborate decoration of Renaissance altarpieces, he developed a principle he designated "necessary richness"[71] and applied it to *Salome* and many other paintings during the remainder of his career. The elaborate architectural setting with its complicated interplay of light and dark derives from Rembrandt, and the detail of the hanging lamp enframed by an arch may well have been taken from one of the Rembrandt reproductions Moreau owned (fig. 22). The Salome figure itself was initially inspired by Raphael,[72] but another source was probably Delacroix's dramatically gesturing young oriental dancer in the *Jewish Wedding*, 1839 (fig. 23). Thus, once again, as was his custom, Moreau integrated studies from nature — as the drawing from the model shows (cat. no. 43-46) — with elements borrowed from the Old Masters.

Wide-ranging visual sources prompted the elaborate decoration filling every part of the picture. The skulls and hideous faces, for example, in Salome's costume and on Herod's throne are taken from antiquity and the Renaissance. They contribute to the grotesque tone of the painting. But, new ingredients essential to the interpretation of the painting are the decorative elements taken from Near and Far Eastern sources. These sources inspired the sketches for Salome's jewelry — which Moreau identified as "magic rings and mirrors" and "the mirror of Solomon" (believed to be employed for divination) and he used them to suggest Salome's "occult" power as a sibyl. Salome's noble and divine status is conveyed by her jeweled attire, reminiscent of Indian deities. The orbs, snakes, and wings — details included in her ornamentation — suggest the uraeus, sacred to Egyptian royalty. Her power as an enchantress is further revealed by an Etruscan element:[73] the girdle around her waist in which the heads of bearded men appear literally chained to her body. The nature of Salome's power to enchant is identified by the lotus she carries in her hand, an Indian symbol of female sexuality. The eye-shaped locket hanging from one of her bracelets probably represents the evil eye, capable of damning the object of its gaze. It explains the spell she casts over Herod.

Numerous symbols throughout the painting reinforce the idea of Salome as an enchantress. There is a panther, seated at the lower right, thought to lure men and beasts with the sweetness of its breath. Another alluring, feminine and deadly figure is the Sphinx. Drawn on the panel of the pedestal at the far left, she is shown with her male victim in her clutches. Above Herod is an antique statue of Diana of Ephesus flanked by images of the Persian god Mithras, both fertility symbols echoing the idea of Salome's sexual power. So, too, does the ornamental column, a recurrent decorative element in painting of the 1860s with phallic overtones usually associated with a victorious male figure. This symbol of male sexual energy is now a minor decorative detail in a scene devoted to a female figure. With it Moreau exemplifies an essential feature of the fatal woman theme as it was used in the nineteenth century: the female's assumption of the sexual dominance traditionally associated with the male.[74]

The profusion of symbols and ornamental details and the complex interplay of light and shadow create a strange ambiance made still more mysterious by the inclusion of certain "irrational" elements, particularly Salome's unnatural stance. Balancing upon her toes, she seems suspended in mid air. Her figure does not appear to be in motion, yet her scarf floats behind her. It is as if an inexplicable draft coming from somewhere beneath the scarf blows it upward, just as it did the robes in the *Athenians* and in *Young Man and Death*. In contrast, heavily bejeweled robes seem to anchor the floating figure of Salome.

In the entire painting there is only one human gesture — that of Salome extending her arm. The only other gesture is that of the statue of Diana whose arms extend above the seated Herod. These gestures establish a visual parallel between the two figures which in turn suggest a similarity in their meaning. Except for these gestures, the figures are as rigid as if they were in a "tableau vivant." Herod and the executioner, who stands to the right, face straight ahead, glancing at Salome only from the corners of their eyes. Though entranced with the dramatic and expressive possibilities of his theme, Moreau totally denied himself the possibility of relying on a naturalistic narrative method. Rather, he used static, "irrational" imagery to create a mysterious and exotic ambiance.

Salome marks a strong stylistic change in Moreau's oeuvre. It was the first time he chose to fill a large and extremely complicated space with a number of small figures. This new format coincided with his movement away, for the most part, from a heavy reliance on antiquity[75] and his shift to the radically new sources mentioned above for his compositions, figures, and accessories. At this time also he began using complex plays of light and dark and gleaming color to create a sense of opulence within the firm, clear structure of the painting. This is especially evident where light strikes an object and overwhelms its details. The result is that the forms lose their definition, becoming ambiguous shapes when viewed from close up, coming into focus when seen from a distance (e.g. the hanging lamp on the right). The surface of the painting is generally lavish, with glittering white touches and specks of intense color emphasized by the monochromatic background.

Salome was Moreau's attempt to create a perfect synthesis of line and color. As his thinking about the conception of the picture as a whole became more rigorous, he executed a series of drawings and oil sketches to serve as experimental compositions. He already had begun, in the early 1870s, to employ a new technique for sketching — first working freely with color and then adding outlines only after his initial idea had been established. The result was that in the finished works prepared from these sketches there were deep, more complicated spatial settings and stronger overall compositions which allowed the eye to travel greater distances between the figures. The most striking result, however, was a new emphasis on value relationships which previously had not been particularly important to Moreau (cat. no. 47). His new treatment of light and dark, so used in *Salome,* contributed greatly to the painting's atmospheric and spatial effects and added to the general mysteriousness of the work. Yet, the emphasis on value relationships never caused Moreau to abondon fully his concern for the precise definition of objects — an obsession he shared with nineteenth-century academic art. He continued to draw in certain details with a very hard and strong line, marking each as clearly as possible. In *Salome* these two different techniques

co-exist, creating a sense of oscillation between elements which are precise and those which are amorphous. Indeed, this oscillation, which fights the stasis of the figures, is the visual basis for the evocative, mysterious power of the painting.

Salome is tantalizing in part because it seems to represent an exclusively personal interpretation of a scene, yet to possess a degree of historical accuracy. An eclectic combination of precisely identifiable details from many different sources, *Salome* is nonetheless not an archaeological reconstruction.[76] Moreau was interested in the decorative elements he borrowed from his sources because they helped him create an imaginary setting which suited his thematic content. His fusion of them was purely personal, without historical precedent. But he did rely on research and his knowledge of other art to provide an *aura* of authenticity to his setting.

Moreau no doubt wanted the viewer to be tantalized by the thought that perhaps the scene did reconstruct the original event with a degree of accuracy, and he used specific symbols to pinpoint the painting historically. The statues of Diana and Mithras, for example, were worshipped in the Roman Empire at the turn of the millenium, precisely when Salome was supposed to have danced before Herod. They, therefore, establish the temporal context of the event and also introduce an element of paganism. The fact that symbols employed in the painting bring together motifs from the East and the West is also relevant in this regard. Jerusalem, the city where the event was supposed to have occurred, was actually the crossroads between the Oriental world and the Roman Empire.

Once again in *Salome* Moreau synthesized a broad spectrum of sources and approaches in order to move the imagination. As he had before, Moreau named Poussin as his model for creating a picture which represented a poetic and imaginary vision of an historical event (III, 4-5). The clarity of visual interpretation of this event, however, in no way diminishes the picture's "mysterious" quality. Although Moreau once again employed allegory with its strictly defined symbols, he established a realm so different and foreign from any identifiable place that the effect was far more evocative than didactic. Also, the great proliferation of decorative elements makes it impossible to be certain whether each detail is symbolic or merely decorative, or both.

"Mysteriousness" is such a key ingredient of this picture that it is valuable to be familiar with Moreau's use of this term. He discussed it in relation to what he considered his primary goal; "abstraction," a term he used to designate the opposite of human sentiments and passions. He equated abstraction with "intuition" which he considered the only reliable basis for painting. "Intuition" he defined as that which it is impossible to explain rationally. Moreau considered intuitions to be spiritual and that when given an effective visual form the result would be magical and even sublime (III, 7, 8). He had a deep belief in the evocative power inherent in the formal elements of painting which he thought capable of transmitting even the most subtle and sophisticated intuitions. Moreau's definition of "abstraction," then, reveals his basic mysticism and explains why he found a symbolic method so appealing for his art. In his oft quoted declaration of faith he stated: "I believe only in what I cannot see and only in what I feel. My brain and reason seem ephemeral and doubtful to me; my interior feeling seems the only thing that is eternal and incontestably certain (IV, 20).

22.

Henri Regnault, 1843-1871
Salome, 1870
Oil on canvas
63 x 40⁷⁄₁₆ in. (160.0 x 102.7 cm.)
The Metropolitan Museum of Art,
New York
22.
Photograph of Rembrandt engraving
*Jesus Chasing the Money Changers
from the Temple*
Musée Gustave Moreau, Paris

23.
Eugene Delacroix, 1798-1863
Jewish Wedding in Morocco, 1839
Oil on canvas
41⁵⁄₁₆ x 55⁵⁄₁₆ in. (105.0 x 140.5 cm.)
Musée du Louvre, Paris

24.
Gustave Moreau
Study for *Salome,* ca. 1872
Wooden mannequin covered with clay
H. 19½ in. (49.5 cm.)
Musée Gustave Moreau, Paris

25.
Gustave Moreau
Head of Hercules
Clay maquette
H. 7¼ in. (18.4 cm.)
Musée Gustave Moreau, Paris

26.
Gustave Moreau
The God of War
Pencil on paper
7⅝ x 5¾ in. (19.4 x 14.6 cm.)
Musée Gustave Moreau, Paris
▶

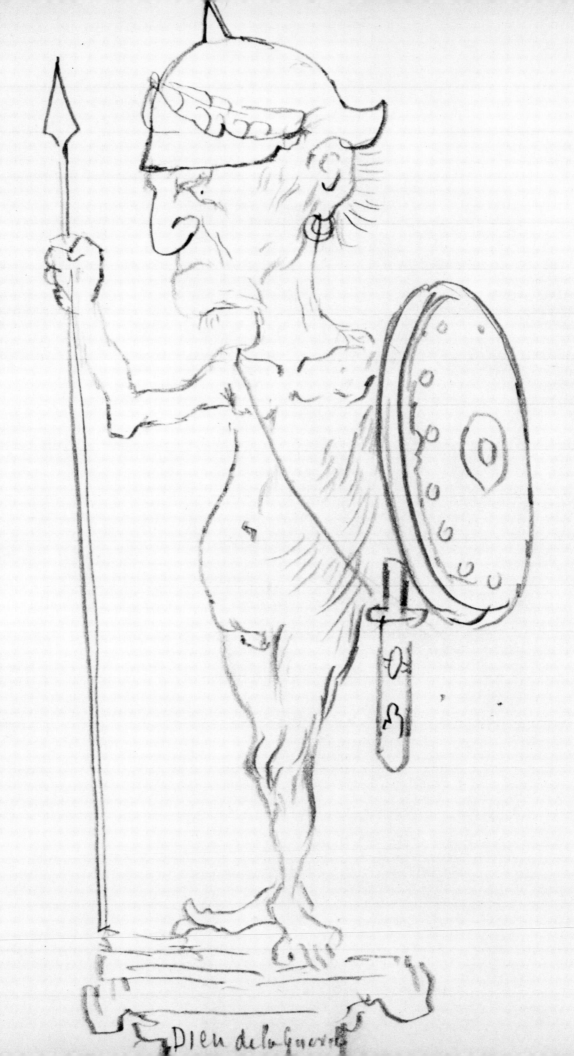

Dieu de la guerre

This statement is at one extreme of Moreau's speculations. If it were all that he had said, it would be difficult to understand why study and careful thought were so much a part of his art. His belief in feeling, however, was coupled with a confidence in its antithesis, reason. His dilemma was a recognition that imagination had to be accompanied by reason to produce great art. It was his self-imposed burden that he felt called upon to combine what he called his limitless imagination with his almost maniacal critical sense (IV, 61). In this regard, Moreau shared a problem with his more traditional contemporaries. It was a problem which arose when he tried to reconcile what seemed to be equally valid but contradictory points of view — Classicism, which emphasized linearity and rational thought, and Romanticism which valued unbridled imagination and often a freer use of color. The conflict grew out of his academic training at the Ecole. There spontaneity and initial inspiration, equated with imagination, were considered appropriate for the preparatory stages of a work of art. Intelligence and technical precision, on the other hand, were to be employed for the highly finished works intended for exhibition. During the course of the nineteenth century there was a gradual change in the evaluation of the sketch, however. It ceased to be considered merely a preliminary step and gained acceptance as a complete work in its own right. This change corresponded to a philosophical shift in which the Neo-Classical tyranny of reason subsided and more respect was accorded to emotion.

Moreau's painstaking labor on *Salome* was rewarded, for the painting was a great critical and public success. By the mid 1870s Moreau's art had not only won him a wider audience, but admiration in literary circles as well. The aesthetic climate in France was changing, and Symbolism would soon emerge. Moreau's art could be best understood by other artists and literary men who were rebelling against Naturalism and its underlying positivistic philosophy. An example was the writer Huysmans who immortalized Moreau's *Salome* in his *A Rebours*, 1884, and certainly fully comprehended the nature of Moreau's *femme fatale* as well as the essentially symbolic nature of the picture. Yet, even so, he paid undue attention to Salome's physical appeal, and when he described her, she became much more physically tempting than she actually is in the painting.

A connection exists between Moreau's imaginative combining of precise images and the way images were used by his contemporaries, the Parnassian poets, Théodore de Banville and Leconte de Lisle. The synthetic style of *Salome* may also owe a debt to Ménard, whose interest in mythology had previously influenced Moreau. Ménard, who was associated with the Parnassians, urged the artists of his time toward greater feats of synthesis. Several of the Parnassians, recognizing the relationship between their art and Moreau's, sent him complimentary copies of their works.[77] Others used his art as a source of inspiration. Another poet whose early work was published under the aegis of the Parnassians and whose work Moreau knew was Baudelaire. The mysterious element in Moreau's work is reminiscent of Baudelaire's belief that the evocative function of art is far more important than its formal precision. In terms of his idealism and intellectual approach, however, Moreau seems closer to Mallarmé. But, the connections are endless. Because of its variety, Moreau's art bears some general relationship to every major current in French letters of his day.[78]

A discussion of *Salome* introduces an important aspect of Moreau's middle period — his sculpture — to which he turned in earnest in the 1870s. In the sixties he had worked with clay while preparing for *Oedipus.* The models for *Salome,* however, are the first extant examples of this sculpture. In a drawing for *Salome* (cat. no. 48) inscribed "après le mannequin" the reference is to the type of small wooden figure with movable joints that still can be purchased in any art supply store. Moreau coated such a figure in clay and dressed it with pieces of cloth (fig. 24) to study the fit of the costume. The drawing indicates that the figure was suspended from strings, which must account for Salome's floating quality in the finished oil.

Moreau also constructed maquettes, or small clay models, to prepare for his pictures. Twelve of them are preserved in the Moreau Museum (fig. 24). In a note he explained that modeling the figures in clay was the first stage in his conception of a new picture,[79] and he felt that these maquettes best revealed his skill with rhythm and the general movement of a composition, which he called its "arabesque,"a feature clearly evident in one of his variants for *Salome* (cat. no. 49). This interest in sculpture made an important contribution to his new style, primarily freeing him to conceive an idea without becoming preoccupied with precise finish.

Moreau's interest in confrontation was constant. It is evident in *Salome* and it attracted him to the theme of his next major work, *Hercules and the Hydra of Lerna* (Salon of 1876, cat. no. 50). In this painting the confrontation is between one of Moreau's characteristic nude adolescent heroes, graceful and static, and his opponent. The antagonist is no longer disguised as a mild slumbering young woman, or the innocent Medea, but appears as the fully monstrous, powerful Hydra with violently twisting coils and hissing heads.

Moreau employed his standard repertory of symbols and his new interest in light to suggest the power possessed by the adolescent Hercules who is tense, controlled, wide-eyed, and alert for any aggressive move his opponent might make. He is clearly a confident hero. His eventual victory, implied by the laurel leaves in his left hand, is visually reinforced by the fact that Hercules occupies the most brightly lit part of the canvas. Lighting functions in other ways, too. It creates an association between the sky — the source of divine power — Hercules, and the victim lying horizontally below the Hydra. The lighting suggests a narrative possibility: that the death of the supine figure will be avenged when Hercules destroys the beast. Moreau also used light and dark to suggest a symbolic restatement of the confrontation between Hercules and the Hydra when he placed the dark cloud in front of the sun. Finally, light unifies the picture by bringing the various spatial levels into a single visual configuration.

In this painting Hercules possesses the characteristics usually associated with an Apollonian solar divinity. His pose, in fact, is based on the *Apollo Belvedere,* the best known antique statue of Apollo. Moreau's transformation of this image included the addition of an assertive stride and an alteration of the position of the arms. The Hydra, Hercules' enemy, parallels Apollo's great antagonist, Python, a serpent personifying the dark underworld forces Apollo had to defeat to establish his oracle at Delphi. It was Louis Ménard who inspired Moreau to make the association between Hercules and Apollo, the Hydra and Python.[80] And, the fact that Moreau produced an *Apollo and Python* in which the appearance and pose of the youthful Apollo resemble that of Hercules in this painting (cat. no. 51) is further evidence that he was aware of these parallels.

From Egyptian art Moreau borrowed the form of the snake which serves as the vertical axis of the Hydra and which in its lack of motion contrasts with the other twisting reptilian forms that seem grafted to it. Moreau wrote that these secondary heads are the physical expression of the reptile's passion (II, 82). He also sketched live snakes, and ultimately his image was the product of combining actual observation with imagery taken from past art. For the detail of the isolated leg at the lower left and the clenched hand just above the waist of the horizontal figure in the mid-foreground, he recalled *Oedipus.* The rocky landscape background, with its distant "peep-hole," is taken directly from Leonardo, while the most prominent of the contorted victims surrounding the Hydra is reminiscent of Poussin's *Echo and Narcissus* (Louvre, ca. 1631) and also Degas' *The Misfortunes of the City of Orleans* (Louvre, 1865). The other figures in the painting recall Romantic subjects. The monstrous creature at the lower right gripping and biting a rock, for example, alludes to the figure on the left-hand side of Delacroix's *Barque of Dante* (Louvre, 1822). The many nude figures in the foreground acknowledge such important earlier pictures as Doyen's *Miraculous Cure of the Plague* (1767) in the Parisian church of St. Roch,[81] Géricault's *Raft of the Medusa* (Louvre, 1817-1819) and Gros' *Napoleon at Jaffa* (Louvre, 1804). The many dying or suffering figures at the lower right and left relate stylistically to Moreau's own art of the 1850s in which there were strong contrasts of light and dark and in which a minimum of rapid brushstrokes created the figural forms.

Hercules, like *Salome,* reflects Moreau's new style of the 1870s, and in both of these paintings the setting has gained in importance; more attention has been given to light, smaller figures — and a greater number of them — have been utilized, and in general a richer variety of techniques have been employed. Moreau's exploration of the symbolic and formal potentials of light is just one sign of his increased sensitivity to the expressiveness of painting's technical means. His drawings for these compositions also reveal a new interest in overall tonal effects and in the disposition of the major forms (cat. nos. 52-54).

Many of the formal devices employed in *Hercules and the Hydra* are intended to strengthen the dichotomy between the main figures. The large, rocky masses of the background landscape, for instance, serve as visual extensions of the two contfronting forces. And, while behind the graceful, stable Hercules there is a smooth, solid element, behind the convoluted profile of the Hydra there is a jagged and complicated form. The contorted shapes of the Hydra's victims, moreover, are a repetition of the Hydra's own convoluted shape.

To suggest that the struggle is spiritual rather than physical, Moreau once again utilized a method of stasis, depriving his imagery of all sense of motion. He pitted a figure with obvious physical strength against a blatantly dangerous foe and yet removed any hint of action from the scene. Thus, the action became latent — totally potential — and Moreau made it possible for the spectator to employ his imagination to fill in the missing drama. The figures, then, are more symbols standing for concepts than actors in a drama, and the image of

Hercules and the Hydra takes on a universal significance.

By endowing an image of physical strength, Hercules, with the traits of the youthful god of light and spirit, Apollo, Moreau gave his image an additional infusion of Idealism. Hercules, the archetype for man facing apparently insurmountable odds, must have had personal significance for Moreau who perhaps experienced such obstacles as self-doubt, and the inhibiting effects of negative criticism of his art. But, this struggle with which Moreau identified is one common to all of mankind, and thus his painting has a universal relevance.

Hercules and the Hydra may also have reflected the specific political situation in France in the 1870s. A dated drawing in the Moreau Museum reveals that the inspiration for this subject came to Moreau in 1869, a critical moment in French history. The Franco-Prussian War, which began the following year, prompted some pointed allegory from artists who normally eschewed reference to contemporary events in their work.[82] Moreau was certainly not immune to the force of these events, and his picture may be interpreted as a statement in which France is symbolized by Hercules, Prussia by the Hydra. The large central snake may represent Bismarck, and the many other snake heads the various German princes he controlled. There is evidence of Moreau's concern with contemporary politics in a caricature he did of *The God of War* in which Bismarck is shown shorn of his moustache (fig. 26).[83] His patriotic attitudes and interest in world events also emerges in his correspondence. For example, there is a letter in which he violently objected to having one of his pictures included in the international exposition of Vienna, 1873, because the Germans had also been invited.[84]

Jean Cassou, in his preface to the catalog of the Louvre exhibition of 1961, discussed Moreau's relationship to his own culture.[85] He hypothesized that Moreau's "strange" paintings are best explained by the mundane life-style characteristic during the Second Empire and Third Republic. Moreau's art expresses the repressed dreams of this business-oriented, restrained, and conservative society. His work was an escape mechanism of a kind, but it also retained certain characteristics of this bourgeois world. It had a clarity and legibility. It was produced in a careful, time-consuming manner, and the reading of the imagery, similarly, required a slow and logical thought process to unravel the meaning. In short, Moreau's artistic method was characterized by the same plodding, methodical, positivistic approach which set the tone of the lives of his public.

Because Moreau was very much a man of his time he created pictures for the purpose of escaping from his society. He wanted to liberate his fellow man, to create spiritual dramas with personal and universal significance. It is impossible to understand all that is evocative and mysterious in Moreau's art without also recognizing its rational, practical, and even trite features. On every level of Moreau's art contradictory elements co-existed. Its basic methodology was sometimes prosaic and sometimes imaginative, its technique at times very polished and controlled and at other moments extremely loose and free. Moreau rebelled against the civilization of his day, yet, in retrospect, is quite representative of it.

Religious Subjects

Moreau's interest in religious themes for his exhibition pictures peaked in the 1870s. The large number of such subjects at this time (they also appear in Moreau's oeuvre in general and altogether account for twenty percent of his total production) is at first glance surprising in a man who was so devoted to mythology. But, it was precisely the same spiritual quest which had motivated his exploration of mythology that in the 1870s first led him to explore religion as subject matter. Both religious literature and religious art dealt directly with the same transcendental issues and existential dilemmas that were at the heart of Moreau's use of mythology. Moreau, for example, had chosen the mythological figure of Orpheus to express the artist's isolation and even destruction by an unresponsive society. He could equally well have employed the image of a religious martyr, as he later did using the figure of Saint Sebastian. Furthermore, the crucifixions and entombments Moreau favored were such clear statements of the dilemma of the creative artist that he was often able to employ this imagery without adding the complex symbolic details he usually relied on. His personal beliefs and values corresponded exactly with the meaning found in the stories from the Old and New Testament.

Most of Moreau's religious works were small oils, painted in subdued colors, often on panels. In them he depicted scenes from the lives of saints or Christ, and, as in *Calvary* (cat. no. 55), expressed a direct and traditional religious spirit. Such religious pictures occurred throughout Moreau's career, never undergoing any stylistic or chronological development. But, there were also times when Moreau felt forced to take certain liberties with his religious images, altering their traditional themes into symbolic ones which would more clearly express his ideas. In one case, *Saint Sebastian* (Salon of 1876) (cat. no. 56), he even borrowed compositional elements from one of his earlier non-religious works, *Young Man and Death*. As in that painting, he wished to express a belief about the creative artist. He, therefore, decided once again to place a standing male figure in the foreground and a second figure behind him on a diagonal. The staring eyes and ornamental detail further distinguish this work from Moreau's usual religious subjects which were typically smaller and quieter.

As revealed in the drawing included here and the final painting, Moreau portrayed the saint as a graceful figure, neither wounded nor disfigured. He represents an ideal whose physical perfection is the outward manifestation of his perfect spirituality. Moreau reduced the signs of physical torture, choosing instead to stress the saint's spiritual calm. This he reinforced by placing the angel in close proximity to the figure of Sebastian. Implicit in the image is the equation of the martyr's spiritual dedication, which enables him to forget his wounds, and the poet's aesthetic idealism, which helps him withstand the worldly pressures attacking his spirit.

The most symbolic religious canvas of Moreau's career is *Jacob and the Angel* (1878) (fig. 28 and the water color, cat. no. 57). In the Old Testament story (Genesis: 32:25-31) Jacob struggles valiantly with the angel to secure his blessing. Moreau wrote that the story expresses the futility both of man's confrontation with the Divine and of his attempt to understand the sacred mysteries of life which God through his angel is able almost effortlessly to prevent. Yet, God looks favorably upon man's efforts and through love fills Jacob with eternal enlightenment (II, 45).

Moreau was not the only nineteenth-century artist to use this theme. Victor Hugo saw the Jacob story as symbolic of personal conflict.[86] And, Delacroix too used it in his St. Suplice murals. But, where Delacroix emphasized the physical aspect of the struggle, Moreau transformed it into a symbolic, spiritual confrontation ultimately revealing divine beneficence.

In Moreau's painting the figures of Jacob and the angel express total concentration. But, while both are static and self contained, their postures differ greatly. Jacob's stance signifies determination; his tense body strains, stretches, and pulls as he exerts all his strength; even his hair flies out behind him from the effort. In contrast, the angel's posture is calm and tranquil; its raised arm rests against a conveniently placed tree stump; its eyes are wide open like that of an iconic figure. The poses suggest that Jacob never actually touches nor sees the angel; he only senses the celestial force represented by this figure. The absence of an actual physical struggle indicates that the battle is a completely spiritual one.

The only clearly symbolic device in this painting is the cloud-crossed orb in the sky, repeated from Hercules. There is no literary or Biblical precedent for this image, which Moreau used as a visual analogue for the connection between Jacob and the angel. The circular shape of the moon echoes the resplendent halo of the brightly-lit angel, and the cloud — a horizontal form passing in front of the moon — parallels Jacob's pose as he thrusts his arms horizontally in front of the angel.

As in Young Man and Death and Prometheus, Moreau uses drapery to accent the hero's genitals and thereby to express Jacob's sensuality. The angel, characteristically, is sexless, which suggests that sexuality must be annihilated if the divine is to be achieved. This suggestion is congruent with Moreau's Neo-Platonic theory and particularly with his statement that the artist can only escape his earthly sensibilities and achieve the realm of divine passion by employing stoic restraint. Only then can he produce a universal statement capable of ennobling and transfiguring the human soul (III, 120).

In Jacob Moreau deals once again with a theme that became almost habitual with him: the confrontation of matter and spirit. But, in his commentary on this work he made a statement which was quite new for him, writing that divine love provides a solution to life's basic problems, that mystical revelation resulting from divine beneficence and conversion helps man understand the basic existential conundrums (II, 45).

In his commentary on King David (Universal Exhibition, 1878) (cat. no. 58), Moreau echoes this thought but adds a new element. Basing his painting on the Old Testament story of King David, he created an image in which the king sits on his throne with a small winged figure at his feet. The basic meaning Moreau wished this scene to communicate was that salvation resulted from divine beneficence, and the new element was that a crisis in creativity could be solved by the divinely inspired power of art.

Of this scene Moreau wrote that the sad King has arrived at the end of his life, and, feeling that he has exhausted all the possibilities of his poetic art, he contemplates his artistic and physical mortality. Seated despondently in an isolated environment which may symbolize the "ivory tower," he is comforted by the music of a lyre played by the angel (which symbolizes poetic genius). The music consoles him with the promise of immortality and God's divine love. Moreau wanted the picture to express the suffering endured by poets and thinkers during moments of discouragement and sadness, and the angel's presence signifies that, despite the pain, there is permanent value in artistic endeavors (II, 55-56; III, 77). The mood of the painting in quiet and melancholy, probably because King David, like Jacob, expressed Moreau's own moments of doubt. But, despite its tone, the work is basically an assertion that the power of art is greater than personal despondency.

Saint Cecilia (cat no. 59) is similar to David and was intended as its pendant (II, 95). In both pictures, one of Moreau's recurrent idealized figures appears — alone and in a state of profound concentration. It was significant to Moreau that in one of the pictures, the figure depicted is that of a young person in reverie, while in the other it is an old person engaged in melancholy contemplation (II, 95). Yet, the two, although they represent chronological opposites, are united by the fact that they are both depicted experiencing a mysterious sorrow and a celestial vision. In the Saint Cecilia the time is evening, and as the melancholy young woman listens to the celestial voice of the cherubim, she senses her impending martyrdom which will be at once tragic and glorious (II, 95).

Moreau thought that he had managed to communicate the religious character of Saint Cecilia by his manipulation of the color tonalities, value relationships, and by the principle compositional elements (II, 96). He seems to have been implying that a particular way of using composition and color could awaken responses similar to those felt during a religious experience. So committed was he to the evocative power of the formal devices available to him in painting, that he considered his written elucidations worthless should the painting itself fail to evoke a response in each spectator (II, 96).

This faith in the expressive power of formal means is a basic aspect of Moreau's art theory, and he reiterated it several times in his notes (III, 54, 57). In the case of Saint Cecilia, he was led to verbalize his belief when his patron requested an explanation of the picture. In response, Moreau asserted that his pictures did not need verbal elucidations. By so stating, he took a stance in opposition to the nineteenth-century public's demand for clear narrative. Form and color could provide sufficient clarity, Moreau thought.[87]

The Silver Age, Orpheus, Morning, Inspiration is one of the ten panels comprising the Ages of Man, a religious work conceived in the late 1870s.[88] The individual oils in this group are not all in the same style; some are very precise, their lines sharp and hard; others appear to be free oil sketches. The conception behind them, however, is completely unified, while also the most complicated and elaborate that Moreau ever created.

Moreau discussed this complex work in a detailed note (II, 87-89). The image is arranged in three rows with three panels in each, and the whole is capped by a large, arch-shaped canvas. The panels simultaneously express Moreau's ideas about the life cycle of the individual man, the artist, and civilization as a whole. His imagery is taken from the Bible and mythology. He employs the figures of Adam, Orpheus, and Cain; the times of day: morning, afternoon, and night; the stages of life: birth, maturity, and death.

Moreau wished to show that the same pattern occurs on a personal and on a universal level. Specifically, the first row contains images representing Adam. In the first, he prays; in the next he is in ecstasy before nature; and in the third he is asleep. Orpheus is the theme of the second row. First he receives inspiration; second he sighs; and third he cries in disillusionment. The third row is the story of Cain and Abel. First Abel sows the seed grain; second he thanks God for the harvest, the fruit of his work; and third Cain kills Abel. Thus, the panels represent from left to right: youth, maturity, old age, and death; and from top to bottom: the Golden Age (of primitive man), the Silver Age (of the beginning of civilization), and the Iron Age (of civilization at its moment of maturity). When the panels are read vertically, not only do they narrate the stages of civilization, but they also reveal increasingly "trying" examples best characterized as birth (Adam's prayer, Orpheus' inspiration, Abel's sowing), maturity (Adam's ecstacy, Orpheus' song, Abel's prayer), and death (Adam's sleep, Orpheus' tears, and Abel's death). The only escape from this eternal cycle is seen in salvation through religious faith, and this is represented by the image of a crucified Christ being supported by angels, in the topmost panel.

The oil sketch depicts Orpheus receiving inspiration. On the temporal level, it represents the morning phase of the day; in terms of the human life span, birth; and in terms of civilization, the Silver Age.

His desire to express his thinking as clearly as possible led him to paint captions under each work stating as precisely as he could the idea underlying this large project. Such a desire for clear exposition appears to contradict his own symbolic method, but it corresponds to his use of allegory as well as his willingness to write commentaries on his paintings — usually for his deaf mother, but for unfortunate patrons as well. A drive toward a unified intellectual statement caused him to combine sacred and profane themes — to take the first step in the direction of the new and still more comprehensive approach which came to dominate his later work.

Fables

Artists, critics, and art historians alike have acclaimed Moreau's *Fables of La Fontaine* as one of the high points of his oeuvre (cat. nos. 63, 65-71).[89] Rouault praised them highly, and when the first twenty-five of them appeared on exhibition in 1881, even a hostile critic was won over:

Of all the painters who collaborated for these illustrations only one tried to do something new: Gustave Moreau . . . despite all that is false and conventional in his art, despite the inevitable heaviness that his repeated retouches produce, one must recognize that the artist has left the beaten path and produced a group of works that are personal, powerful and new as ideas and skillful in technique. His are the most complete works in this exhibition.[90]

Moreau probably accepted the commission for this series because the fables appealed to him as emblematic narratives. Since their symbolic value had already been firmly established, he simply had to concentrate on developing new imagery for them. Moreau knew that there were writers who had adapted the fables to express personal, esoteric philosophies,[91] and he was fully determined to make his own treatment of them neutral. Moreover, since his commission entailed a large number of pictures, he had to produce approximately one every two weeks and, therefore, did not have time to evolve the multi-leveled symbolism characteristic of much of his previous work.

Despite the fame of these watercolors, they were only seen *in toto* in 1886 and 1906, and many of them are purportedly lost today. Enough evidence exists, however, to reconstruct the history of the series, and an approximate chronology can be established for the sixty-four Fables. (see Appendix I).

Anthony Roux, an art dealer and collector from Marseille, was responsible for commissioning the series, in 1879, from a number of then prominent artists, including Moreau.[92] Although what motivated his interest in La Fontaine's fables is not known, it must have bordered on the obsessive since it was contagious enough to be passed on to his nephew, Alfred Baillehache.[93]

After the first exhibition of Roux's fables in 1881, which included Moreau's twenty-five watercolors, Roux asked him to continue working until he had produced sixty-four watercolors in all. Since Roux mostly chose world-renown *animaliers* such as Rosa Bonheur and Gérôme for the project, he must have been particularly impressed by the variety in Moreau's work to have wished him to continue. Moreau acquiesced to Roux's request because of the critical acclaim the first twenty-five illustrations had won him, and also because he must have enjoyed working rapidly and exploiting the surprising effects created by the fluid watercolor medium. Moreau even went so far as to confess that he felt he only painted really well when he painted rapidly (III, 63). Also, he must have appreciated this opportunity to exercise his visual imagination without feeling compelled to make a major philosophical statement. This commission, then, was different from anything he had done before, and he concentrated a large part of his energy on color and design. The result was not only the libration of his color sense, but the creation of the most spirited works in his oeuvre. The critics immediately took note of this freshness when the complete series was exhibited in 1886 at Goupils.[94]

While Moreau achieved a new degree of freedom in this series, he also, of course, continued to build upon his previous experiences and to follow his usual painstaking technical procedures. His first step was to go to the botanical garden and the Museum of Natural History to sketch skeletons and animals (cat. nos. 60-62). Having regained a familiarity with the denizens of the animal world, he made a large number of studies of the specific animals included in the fables which concerned him. He then produced a complete sketch for each subject. Some of these are very free (cat. no. 70), others precise and schematic (cat. no. 65), but all are complete ideas for detailed watercolors. As there is only one sketch for each of La Fontaine's narratives, and most of the ideas are straight-forward, simple illustrations of the literary source, Moreau must have conceived them all without hesitation.

The research Moreau conducted before starting a single composition and his careful anatomical studies are evidence of his having been influenced by the inductive method of nineteenth-century science. Moreau's starting point was a belief in, and a reliance upon, observable fact. Even if in his theoretical writings he rails against such a viewpoint as the aim of art, and even though many of his own illustrations for the fables move beyond this approach to become imaginative statements, his link with the prevalent positivism of the ninteenth century is clearly detectable.

Phoebus and Boreas (cat. no. 63), one of the first of the illustrations, was finished by July 7, 1879. In this vivid sketch, Moreau manipulated scale, value, and hue to create an extremely dramatic effect, making the figure of the god gigantic and overpowering and those of the humans below insignificant and cowering. The image contains strong light and dark contrasts, and the dominant impression is created by the use of brilliant red and yellow. In the finished watercolor, form and color are used to create the same dramatic effect which sets the tone for the best of Moreau's fables.

Although not exhibited here, there is a group of fables characterized by monochromatic settings and still figures which produce a sense of calm, which permeates a number of the fables for example in *The Miser and the Monkey*.[95] Until this time such a mood of tranquility had been evident only in some of Moreau's religious subjects and landscape studies.

In this group of quiet fables, Moreau came as close to Realism as he would ever get. A slight tendency toward a direct observation of nature also became most evident during this period when Moreau was working for Roux. For example, if the drawing for one of the additions he made to *Hercules and the Daughters of Thestius* (1882) (cat. no. 64) is compared with a preliminary study he did in the 1850s (cat. no. 14), it becomes apparent that Moreau came to base his work more directly upon the model during the 1880s.

The Dragon with Many Heads and the Dragon with Many Tails (cat. no. 65) reveals both the strength and weakness of this set of watercolors. The sketch is drawn with a strong, precise, unvacillating line which indicates that Moreau was able to express his initial inspiration confidently. The composition repeats the standard formula which balances a foreground against a distant view; and, Moreau also relied on details he had used in previous works, for example, the rocky landscape which he had already used in *Hercules* and which derived originally from Leonardo. This work epitomizes the

27.

27.
Gustave Moreau
Jacob and the Angel, 1878
Oil on canvas
102 x 58½ in. (258.4 x 148.6 cm.)
Fogg Art Museum, Harvard University,
Cambridge

28.
Gustave Moreau
Jupiter and Semele, 1889-95
Oil on canvas
84 x 45 in. (213.2 x 114.3 cm.)
Musée Gustave Moreau, Paris

29.
Gustave Moreau
Copy of a Northern Renaissance
Altarpiece
Pen and ink on tracing paper
4 x 1$^{15}\!/_{16}$ in. (10.2 x 4.9 cm.)
Musée Gustave Moreau, Paris

feature most characteristic of Moreau's fables: his reliance upon past inspiration and simultaneously, his creation of confident and often fresh imagery and compositions.

Moreau's illustration for *The Mogul's Dream* (cat. no. 67) provides insight into the full range of his decorative and orientalizing sensibility. In this instance he created an elaborate, imaginative interior to serve as a setting for a dream. The variety of detail and color in the finished work insures its success even though the imagery is not totally new. The man's pose is taken from Moreau's own *David,* and the little circles above where Moreau would draw the Mogul's dreams are a traditional formulation Moreau borrowed from medieval manuscript illuminations.

Some of Moreau's images are uninspired copies of earlier ideas, simply repeating familiar compositional types, as does for example the Fables' frontispiece which echoes *The Peri,* a drawing included in the Salon of 1866.[96] The compositional formula of *The Dragon* (cat. no. 65), too, is characteristic of many of the fables (cat. nos. 70, 71). It was no doubt because the series was so large that Moreau repeated some basic compositional approaches. One of these was to establish a sense of balance by contrasting the two halves of the image. Foreground elements would occupy one entire side while the other side would depict a deep plunge into space. Used by artists for centuries, an artistic device of this type required no imagination on Moreau's part, and it may have been that he was led to repeat this format so often because the fables themselves tended to be repetitive.

The Peacock's Complaint to Juno (cat. no. 69) shares with the best fables a rhythmic quality and an especially sensitive use of color — in this case it is the delicacy of the blue that is exceptional. The svelte, graceful figure of Juno is used to create a new diagonal compositional format which produces a strong arabesque sweep throughout the work. So strong is this movement that it all but obscures the fact that she is Moreau's standard female type.

The composition for *The Wolf and the Lamb* (cat. no. 70) is new and dramatic and the drawing violent and agitated, strongly contrasting the innocent lamb and the voracious wolf. Moreau uses nature as the vehicle to express a mood, employing a windy, stormy landscape and a bare tree to establish a spikey, agitated play of line across the paper. The sense created by the elements is one of violent foreboding, and this emotional tone effectively sets the scene for the narrative.

If the repetitiveness of some of the compositional types suggests a flagging of talent, Moreau nonetheless deserves full credit for the numerous technical innovations and fresh conceptions in this series. And, despite their weaknesses, the thirty-eight watercolors Moreau created between May 1881 and 1886 are noteworthy for their experimental and delicate use of color, particularly in the finished versions of the fables. A preparatory drawing for *The Frogs Asked for a King* (cat. no. 71) gives a good idea of Moreau's free and light color solutions in the finished versions.

Moreau's treatment of *The Fables of La Fontaine* reveals that when a subject suggested no link with a previous work he could become daring and even brilliant in inventing a new solution. However, some themes reminiscent of his earlier pictures failed to inspire him, and thus he restated old ideas.

The nature of the literary source, moreover, prompted many simple, repetitious compositions. Yet, the high points of the series disclose Moreau's increasing desire to experiment, particularly with color possibilities. Beyond that, the *Fables* reflect the variety of Moreau's art, despite the noticeable moments of flagging creativity. Similarly apparent, but not to be exaggerated either, is the element of realism present in some examples in this commission.

After completing this group of works, Moreau continued to produce watercolors and to explore the potentials of color. The presence of these watercolors in the Moreau Museum today indicates that Moreau did not consider them finished works, but studies for works to be exhibited. However, in some completed compositions, such as *The Toilette,* he did employ extremely strong color harmonies. Today the vibrant and fresh works in which Moreau employed the watercolor medium are the mainstay of his reputation. They are what the public has come to know since they have been the focus of numerous Moreau exhibitions and recent publications.[97] A representative of these works included here is *Hercules and the Doe* (cat. no. 72). A loosely sketched figural composition, the drawing seems little more than a skeleton to which free and flowing color was added. And, works as diverse as *Dante and Virgil* (cat. no. 73), the *Prodigal Son* (cat. no. 74), and *Centaurs Carrying a Dead Poet* (cat. no. 75), although restatements of themes which had preoccupied Moreau years before, are very significant because they served as excuses for Moreau's abandoning himself to the use of bright and fluid color.

Moreau's mature period from 1870 to 1886, then, was characterized by a number of technical innovations and the investigation of new subject matter, particularly Biblical and Oriental. Although he often reverted to earlier compositional solutions, particularly those he had explored during the 1860s, his treatment of them was now profoundly affected by his new, more daring use of color and light-dark relationships. And, he wrote that his artistic experiences had finally taught him to utilize light to create a sense of space in his compositions (for example fig. 8). He was, in fact, so satisfied with the changes in his work that he began to enlarge upon and repaint many of his older, unfinished canvases.

During this period Moreau continued to rely upon literary sources, but there was a new freedom in his use of them. In essence, he became more original and gave himself more latitude to transform the art and literature that stimulated him into personal statements. The result was an increase in scope, with work ranging from the essentially evocative *Salome* to the politically conscious *Hercules,* the spiritually inspired *Orpheus,* and the technically brilliant, but not particularly profound or philosophical, Fables.

However, the major shift that occurred was in the content of Moreau's work. The earlier images, which had highlighted the confrontation of forces and beings representing these forces, were now transformed into images suggesting solutions to man's transcendental dilemmas. Also, Moreau began to make his images more encyclopedic and, therefore, better able to summarize all of his knowledge and experience. As always, he continued to be interested in bringing his art to a coherent conclusion in terms of its philosophical content and style, and ultimately this was the quest which came to dominate the last decade of his life.

By the last decade of the nineteenth century Moreau had become part of the artistic establishment. He replaced Boulanger in the Académie des Beaux-Arts in November 1888 and headed an atelier at the Ecole des Beaux-Arts. Symbolist writers lionized him and sent him books and periodicals, which are now an integral part of his extant library. He was equally admired by the "Decadents"— Huysmans, Robert de Montesquiou, Jean Lorrain — and by the Rosicrucian, Sâr Péladan.

Moreau, however, reacted with hostility to much of this admiration. He refused Sâr Péladan's invitation to participate in the *Salon de la Rose + Croix,* an exhibition devoted to religious idealism in painting and with stated aims close to Moreau's own ideological position. He berated these younger men, in his writing, for their posturing, charlatanism, and apparent enthusiasm for dreams and intangibles (IV, 31).

Moreau was a precursor both of the Symbolists and the Decandents. But, he denied that these movements in turn had any influence on his work even though he was undoubtedly affected by the ideology espoused in the various Symbolist books and articles he was sent. He preferred to consider his work the logical culmination of his personal experiences rather than the outgrowth of a new aesthetic movement.

Many of the stylistic and philosophical conceptions that characterized his earlier work appeared again during this late period. In *The Siren and the Poet* (cat. no. 76), for example, Moreau returned to the painting style that he had used in the 1880s, placing large, svelte figures within a very detailed setting. The painting, his most important public commission of this period, was ordered in 1894 for the Gobelin Tapestry Works and then exhibited as a tapestry in the Universal Exhibition of 1900.98 In it, as in many of his earlier works, he portrayed a dominant female and an adolescent male and once again explored the nature of creativity and of woman's role in relation to the creative process.

Motivating the key paintings of this late period was Moreau's desire to utilize a lifetime's experience of working with the technical and philosophical problems of his art to produce pictures more complex than any of his previous works. *The Triumph of Alexander the Great* (cat. no. 77), completed by Moreau in 1892, is the first of these pictures. Filled with innumerable small figures and architectural details, it shows the great Macedonian military ruler seated on a throne with a victory figure standing above him as he receives homage from subjugated oriental princes. The picture dramatizes the point of contact between East and West, and Moreau wrote that for him India represented all that was mysterious and unsettling and the picture showed the triumph of a radiant and superb Greek spirit over unknown regions of mystery and dream (II, 63-64). Thus, the painting, which originated in an attempt to unify a lifetime's study of world art, actually became a declaration of faith in rationality and western culture. But, Moreau must have had second thoughts as to the validity of the painting's philosophical content, for he never completed *The Triumph of Alexander the Great.*

The sketchy state of the painting reflects Moreau's working method and also reveals the function of his controversial "non-objective" oil sketches. The most remarkable aspect of the picture is its carefully drawn details. Moreau's subsequent finished pictures suggest that had this one been fully

elaborated, it would have been filled with very precisely rendered forms. One preliminary drawing for a detail (cat. no. 78) exemplifies the nature of the ornamentation.99 Figures and decorative details are applied over areas of color — unlike the academic method which taught that the drawing came first and the application of color second. Moreau, however, thought of his image in terms of broad areas of tone, and only when the harmonies had been set did he begin to add the particulars of the imagery. Although this technique was not completely new (Moreau had already employed it in studies for *Salome), Alexander* provides the clearest example of its use in a large and complete painting.

Moreau's *Triumph of Alexander the Great* makes it apparent that those of his studies which have been isolated and publicized as precursors of Abstract Expressionism are actually preparatory sketches. Two such examples are a sketch (cat. no. 80) which seems to be a preliminary study for *Jupiter and Semele* and another (cat. no. 81) which appears to be some kind of landscape setting. That such studies are the basis for paintings is proved by a sketch (cat. no. 82) in which a figure is visible. *The Good Samaritan* (cat. no. 83) is also clearly a figurative composition although its relationship to the "subjectless" oils is immediately evident.

While Moreau produced sketches throughout his life, the later sketches took on a different character. In a letter to Fromentin written forty years earlier, he had mentioned that after establishing the basic outline for the figures and the interior modeling of a composition, he then freely applied areas of color. But in the 1870s, when Moreau's technical freedom had increased, he began to eliminate the linear framework. His first idea for a composition now immediately took the form of an oil sketch. However, there is no doubt that Moreau always had figurative compositions in mind, even when he was simply applying strokes and dabs of colored pigment to a canvas. These color areas implicitly contained his pictorial ideas and the seed of the picture's expressive content. While Moreau never intended to create non-objective art, his work nonetheless supports the contention that it influenced the development of Expressionism in the twentieth century.100

In his later years when Moreau was in increasingly ill health and undoubtedly conscious of his impending death, he attempted to make the images he created more deliberate syntheses of his beliefs about life and art. A return to religious subjects occurred in such works as *The Ideal Flower, the Catholic Church* (cat. no. 84). The compositon, dominated by a central form in the shape of a pyramid, is an often-repeated one in Moreau's late compositions such as *Dead Lyres* and *Mystic Flower.*101 In each of these images, a woman, a flower, and a cross rest upon a mound of dead figures. These images provided Moreau with a vehicle for stating that sacrifice and even death are a necessary part of the process leading toward the creation of a poetic or religious ideal.

But Moreau's views were often contradictory, and he did not always idealize death. The subject of one of his late watercolors, *St. John of the Apocalypse* (cat. no. 85), is the cataclysmic end of human life. In it, the saint looks into the distance as though envisioning the future destruction of mankind. The composition, which includes St. John's traditional attribute the eagle and Moreau's habitual ornamental column, is made up of diagonals which produce a sense of instability.

The compositional unrest works with the idea of the Last Judgment which Moreau associated with St. John. A more hopeful attitude is represented by another late watercolor, the *Argonauts* (cat. no. 86), mythological figures Moreau had always interpreted as symbols of youthful confidence.[102] These two late watercolors not only communicate contrasting philosophical positions but also represent Moreau's stylistic extremes. Whereas *St. John* is very carefully drawn, the *Argonauts* is an extremely free sketch. Moreau in his late years persisted in exhibiting only finished works, but both of the styles represented by these watercolors were satisfactory for solving the problems which made the finished works possible.

At this time Moreau was suffering from the stomach cancer which finally caused his death, and he fought his illness by engaging in herculean artistic feats. His belief in the work ethic was so strong that he looked to work for his salvation. One concrete sign of his belief is the proliferation of precisely rendered detail in his late paintings. The most extreme example occurs in *Jupiter and Semele* (1889-1895) (fig. 28), which is at once a summary of and conclusion to Moreau's entire production.[103]

Jupiter and Semele, Moreau's last large finished painting, has as its subject the king of the gods and one of his mortal loves. The mythological episode the painting is based on is that in which Jupiter's jealous wife Juno persuades Semele to ask the god to show himself in his full splendor. Jupiter, bound by an oath to grant Semele's request, complies although he knows that the vision will destroy any mortal. Despite Semele's death in the myth Jupiter manages to save their unborn son Bacchus, hiding him in his thigh until the time of his birth.

An oil sketch (cat. no. 87) of 1889 is a record of Moreau's first idea for this composition. In it Jupiter is enthroned, Semele is on his lap, and Bacchus is flying away from her. Jupiter's attribute, the eagle, is poised below the throne. In this oil sketch Moreau worked with the placement of areas of color, light, and shade; explored compositional possibilities; and experimented with each figure's posture. Of course, he then worked on each specific figure with painstaking drawings (cat. no. 88). Wanting the picture to be full of energy, fluidity, and brilliant color, Moreau explored in sketches the various possible means of achieving these effects.

In the early stages of the picture Moreau began to elaborate upon the theme by adding figures, and each addition altered the traditional meaning of the subject. For example, in one large sketch in the Moreau Museum (no. 808), a figure is added to the left of the eagle at the bottom and Bacchus is shown flying away. Such changes reflect the fact that Moreau used the subject to make a personal statement, and the myth served simply as the starting point for expressing ideas he had been experimenting with during the preceding twenty years. The basic challenge in this work, as in all of Moreau's canvases, was to select imagery and give pictorial form to the ideas he wished to communicate.

In the finished painting Moreau expanded the composition by increasing its width and adding more specific details. This type of expansion, which dealt with value relationships and the overall presentation of the subject, was typical of him. A group of figures added at the bottom served to support all of the sumptuous minutiae in the picture, and along with many of the other newly added elements makes the painting more specifically symbolic and synthetic in character.

Moreau based the composition of *Jupiter and Semele* on one of his copies of a Northern Renaissance altarpiece (fig. 29). From this copy Moreau took the symmetrical balance of the composition, the attendant figures, and the elaborate throne. Both *Jupiter and Semele* and the altarpiece copy are intended to give visual form to a transcendental idea. The altarpiece copy represents the Divinity in terms of the traditional theological tripartite composite of Father, Son, and Holy Spirit, but simultaneously it expresses the oneness implicit in the three parts by enclosing them with the throne. In *Jupiter and Semele* Moreau used another elaborate throne to provide the figures with a similar unity. *Jupiter and Semele* with its three main figures fits neatly into this altarpiece format. Whereas in the altarpiece God is seated on an elaborate throne in the center with Christ on the left and the Alpha-Omega inscribed on the right, in Moreau's painting the enthroned Jupiter is central with Semele on the left and a lyre on the right. The overall pictorial inspiration, then, with its hierarchic scale, symmetry, balance, and precise decoration, derived from the early Renaissance.

Moreau's major departure from the altarpiece model is the figure of Bacchus which was taken from a Dante scene by Flaxman.[104] Flying diagonally away from the two larger figures, Bacchus actually somewhat weakens the composition and deprives the painting of some of the unity which its prototype, the Renaissance altarpiece, enjoyed. The Jupiter figure is based on several sources: a copy he made of an antique fresco, an antique bronze Moreau owned, Ingres' picture of *Jupiter and Thetis, a*nd his own watercolor *Jupiter and the Thunderbolts.* The figure of Semele recalls Moreau's *Phaeton,*[105] 1878, in which a similar pose is used for another figure who dies as a result of Jupiter's power. In this painting, then, Moreau repeatedly relied upon imagery he had used previously in thematically related subjects. In part these repetitions reflect his desire to express his total experience as a painter. But he was now independent enough to transform these images into something new and original.

The lower section of *Jupiter and Semele* is filled with eyes, faces, and forms resembling planetary bodies, all emerging from a dark background. A drawing and inscription for these figures explain that they are all divinities of Death, ruled by Hecate, the goddess of the Moon and Darkness. They are destiny, death, sleep, misery, fraud, age, and discord — all that is pernicious and terrible. Moreau's search for imagery capable of conveying the horrors of life led him to dictionaries of witchcraft and books on world mythology.[106]

Although Moreau's earlier works had been characterized by the complexity of their symbolism, in this picture Moreau expanded his conception of symbolism still further. The figure of Jupiter continues to function as the principle figures did in Moreau's previous paintings, that is, many symbols are used to establish his meaning. But, whereas in the earlier works the principle figures served as the focus for all of the other figures and details, in *Jupiter and Semele* there are many almost equally important figures, and the meaning of each and of all the interrelationships is necessary for an understanding of the total statement made by the picture.

Jupiter, a large and youthful hero, embodies the universal ideal. He holds a lyre which Moreau used to symbolize human intelligence, the attribute which permits genius to attain the ideal (II, 38). A god-hero-poet, he unifies all diversity — even man's sexual duality. Thus, on his chest he wears a lotus, the traditional Indian symbol of the female principle in the universe, while a lingam, representing the Hindu male principle, accompanies his attribute, the eagle. On his chest he also bears the Egyptian symbol of godhead, the scarab, while his foot rests on a snake biting its own tail, a symbol of eternity.

Semele, because she is a woman, represents sensual temptation. And, since Moreau believed that man must rise above his senses to achieve the divine state of spiritual understanding, he chose to imply her destruction. The blood dripping from her side thus signifies her inevitable death.

Bacchus, the child of Jupiter and Semele, is able to escape his mother's fate perhaps because he combines her sensuality/humanity and Jupiter's ideality/divinity. He represents what Moreau considered to be man's condition: a constant conflict between idealistic, spiritual thought and physical, sensual temptation.

Jupiter occupies the upper portion of the picture while the figure seated directly below the eagle is Pan, the most famous divinity inhabiting the earth. The two figures beside Pan represent Death and Suffering. Moreau established the identity of the former with a sword and hourglass and of the latter with a crown of thorns. These three figures — Pan, Death, and Suffering — stand for the realm of earth and human life, and the monsters below them symbolize all the evils that are antithetical to the ideal.

Moreau's writings include two explicit exegeses of the painting, one dating from 1895 and the other from 1897 (IV, 16; II, 41, 44).[107] He wrote of Semele that she was transformed by her vision of the eternal, that its splendor penetrated her so that she died in ecstasy, that divine love killed the earthly love in her (represented by Bacchus). Her fate reflects the transforming effect of any contact with the eternal and divine, and it is an effect sought by every being — even by the denizens of the evil, melancholy, and petrified world below. Semele's death represents an apotheosis and symbolizes the potential immortality of all nature and material existence when transformed by the divine ideal. Thus, the painting makes use of pagan mythology to create an image which communicates what is basically a Christian belief.

Some of the ideas Moreau expressed in his written commentaries, though not visible in this picture, nonetheless are useful for an understanding of his philosophical viewpoint. One such example is the fact that Bacchus is destroyed, and another is Moreau's statement that the picture is based on Christian ideology.

The picture, together with the commentaries, is Moreau's final statement of the problem dealt with in all of his previous paintings and which he called "the great mystery." By this he meant the conflict was between man's sensual nature and the ideal or divine.

The terms Moreau used in his commentaries, as well as his specific statements, are Gnostic-Manichaean in character, emphasizing the conflict between light and dark and the inherent evil of matter which the individual must constantly strive to overcome. There was Gnostic churches active in Paris at this time, and this system of belief influenced other French artists of the day, among them Victor Hugo.[108] However, the likelihood is that the similarity between Moreau's terminology and that of this religious sect was coincidental. After all, Moreau had been concerned with light and dark contrasts since the 1870s, and he had been preoccupied with the subject of good versus evil from the very beginning of his career. That Moreau gradually combined his philosophical and technical concerns is natural, and finding a parallel between his religious philosophy and Gnostic-Manichaeanism may simply have suggested certain pictorial solutions, for instance the lower part of *Jupiter and Semele*. Indeed, his statement most clearly related to a Manichaean vision occurs in his commentary for the painting rather than in the picture itself.

More fundamentally, Moreau's underlying philosophy was Neo-Platonic, as an interpretation of the thinking of Plotinus, the foremost Neo-Platonist, reveals:

Plotinus endeavored to liberate his soul from its fleshly bonds; he wished it to pass beyond the visible world into the ecstasy of union with the invisible which he felt to be the source of all vision and all reality.[109]

However, a connection can be made between Moreau's work in general, and this painting specifically, and a great many of the philosophical positions current in the intellectual and artistic community at the end of the nineteenth century. Certainly, Moreau's use of a synthetic language to make his statement is not an isolated event. It is analogous to the objectives of the Theosophists, who looked to all civilizations for the essential truths although their faith was primarily based on the oriental religions and certain occult beliefs. One of the most popular books to come out of the Theosophical movement was Edouard Schuré's *The Great Initiates* (1889). Though this book is not in Moreau's library, he may have been familiar with it as there are striking similarities to it in his commentaries. Schuré's work contains an allusion to an image of Jupiter on the heights and Hecate in the valleys, and he states that if one removes oneself from the realm of matter, the spirit joins the pure ether of eternal things as does the eagle at Jupiter's throne. Schuré also presents Jesus, and by extension Christianity, as the culmination of hermetic knowledge, and Moreau, too, said that this scene from pagan mythology was essentially Christian. But, there are major differences between Schuré's thinking and Moreau's, and although Moreau may have been somewhat influenced by Schuré's book, it is more likely that the similarities in their works result from their interest in related ideas and their use of similar sources.

Moreau's work, and *Jupiter and Semele* specifically, bears a resemblance to a contemporary artist like Chenavard and also to certain Rosicrucian tendencies in attempting to find a common philosophical truth in all the complex phenomena and thought of the time.[110] Carlos Schwabe's poster for the first Rose-Croix Salon of 1892[111] is reminiscent of Moreau's work in theme. It shows figures emerging from the mud and ascending toward the light.

Similarities can even be found between Moreau's work and Gauguin's. Gauguin, too, used exotic subject matter in an attempt to come to grips with such transcendental questions as man's place in the universe and the general meaning of life. Gauguin's picture *Where do we come from? Who are we? Where are we going?* was painted at approximately the time Moreau was creating *Jupiter and Semele,* and it deals with the same questions that concerned Moreau. Although Gauguin's artistic language could not have been more different, his choice of a complicated symbolic system parallels Moreau's use of symbolism and allegory.

That a similarity existed between Moreau's art theory and late nineteenth-century Symbolist aesthetics has already been mentioned. Unlike the younger Symbolists, however, Moreau did not intend his pictures merely to be unique icons the viewer would contemplate. Rather, the nature of his imagery and his creative method reveal that he considered the primary purpose of his paintings didactic and intended them to assist in the attainment of the ideal.

Moreau never lost his faith in his ability to make an intellectual statement that would be valid for his own age and for the future. Whereas both Moreau and the Symbolists thought of their works as symbolic statements, their methodologies were quite dissimilar. The stylistic touchstone of the late nineteenth-century Symbolists—the Nabis for example —was simplification of form and color often coupled with imagery so vague as to be indistinguishable. Moreau's desire to evoke was combined with a very exact and detailed style, and it is precisely this combination of the evocative and the specific that makes his work unique.

Although Moreau embedded a myriad of allusions within each of his images, he did not expect the reader to research each detail as he himself had done. On the contrary, he assumed the viewer would be able to understand his paintings by reflecting upon their forms and allowing them to awaken responses. This point of view—that the purpose of a work of art is to be evocative—was, in fact, characteristic of the late nineteenth century in general and a reaction against the literal and phenomenon-oriented interpretation of the world set forth by the Naturalists and Impressionists. Nonetheless, Moreau's methodology, in terms of its concern with precision of detail does share some of the values propounded by the Naturalists and Impressionists. But, then, this orientation was also basic to nineteenth-century culture in general, with its rigorous quest for accuracy and truth.

When asked by Leopold Goldschmidt for an explanation of *Jupiter and Semele,* the picture he had just purchased, Moreau provided a commentary but said that he was doing so merely to be agreeable, not because he felt the painting needed one to be understood. The meaning of the painting, he said, resided in its appearance, provided the viewer knew how to "read" a picture. And, he believed that "reading" merely necessitated the ability to dream and to love a little, for these he considered the functions of the imagination.[112] It was his belief in the imaginative and rational faculties of man that pervaded his art theory and that dictated the contents and appearance of his entire oeuvre.

In summary, Moreau's art throughout his oeuvre is characterized by its wide-ranging and eclectic intellectualism and its technical experimentation. Early in his career Moreau accepted the basic tenets of the Romantic school and followed Delacroix in style, subject matter, and philosophy. Thematically his paintings dealt with man's place in the universe and his constant striving to attain the ideal, woman's allure and destructiveness (that is, the power of the *femme fatale),* and the artist's isolation and failure to be understood. He combined these themes with a great respect for tradition and for principles

gleaned from his academic studies and from his observation of Old Master paintings. The variety of Moreau's work, at every moment of his artistic career, is striking. But, his stylistic direction emerges most clearly from a study of the major paintings he exhibited, for these provide a view of the progression of his technical vocabulary.

Moreau's art was based on the premise that his personal interpretation of the world was a more valid source for art than the natural world of phenomena. The major part of his work, early and late alike, adheres to this essentially Neo-Platonic world view which led him increasingly toward religion. Like many late nineteenth-century idealist thinkers, who were appalled by the materialism of their society, Moreau too concluded that Christian mysticism and idealism offered the final solution to his dilemmas.[113] His mature production began with a dualistic vision of human existence, which continued to link him to Romanticism. But, by the 1870s, he had begun to move away from Romantic content to a more syncretistic system (as in *Hercules* and *Jacob,* for instance). The culmination was *Jupiter and Semele* which, like several other of Moreau's late works, basically presented an image of transcendental unity and utilized a method at once allegorical and symbolic.

Moreau saw the world in terms of opposing forces and always utilized the principle of contradiction in his art. But his own actions, too, were often contradictory. For instance, although Moreau had faith in the ability of a painting to speak for itself (IV, 25), he nonetheless wrote explanatory commentaries. And, while he valued unfinished works sufficiently to preserve them in a museum, he only exhibited the finished ones. While he believed that pictures had different meanings for different viewers, he used symbols allegorically, that is attaching specific meanings to them. Technically, he combined two styles, generally considered in opposition to each other: the painterly and the linear. He created images that looked as if they had one meaning, but actually meant the opposite, as in *Oedipus* and *Jacob.* On a personal level, he was alternately repelled and attracted by the world of the senses. In terms of his public life, he retained his separateness from the art establishment, but at the same time was accepted as a member of it. But, none of these examples is as significant as the conflict Moreau experienced between his belief in intuition and his belief in rationality. He moved continuously between these two poles until the resulting oscillation became the key to his art. It was the conflict between these two beliefs which impelled him to create, but which also quite often inhibited the successful realization of his creation.

Moreau was an artist who subscribed to a philosophical viewpoint that denied the validity of the world of the senses, and yet, because painting as an art form depends on the senses, in practice he could not escape from this world. Though he reacted against the positivism and materialism of his age, he was firmly linked to the attitudes and approaches which they produced. Thus, his methodology was careful, painstaking, and dependent upon research, all of which was antithetical to his idealist beliefs. Moreau could not escape the crassness of his culture in his daily life; yet, in his art he could. And, the fact that he chose to produce art so laden with symbolism can be understood as reflecting a need to create an alternative to the world he despised. In a sense, then, Symbolism and Realism can be seen as two sides of the same coin, both being products of the same nineteenth-century values. This may help explain Moreau's interest in nature and landscape and the immediacy of many of his illustrations for the fables of La Fontaine. Although only a small part of his production, they are interesting as a link to the mainstream art activity of the time. Similarly, the existence of political overtones in his work refutes the idea of Moreau as an isolated ivory-tower genius, an image perpetuated by Huysmans.[114] In short, Moreau was not in the least oblivious to the world around him.

Moreau's creation of a personal statement about existence emerged from a synthesis of literary and pictorial sources. Thus, to understand his work fully and to completely grasp its symbolism one must approach his paintings in almost the same scholarly manner in which he created them. But, the paintings retain much of their fascination even if their meaning is not totally transparent. They have a unique vitality and the power to affect each viewer in a unique manner. Their color and lyricism make them visual experiences that arouse curiosity even when nothing more is known about them. They appeal to the intellect and to the intuition, the two faculties Moreau moved between.

Moreau's significance lies not only in his art, but in his teaching as well. However, because he believed so strongly in his students' freedom and because he was so eclectic, he had little specific stylistic influence on the art of his time. Rather, it is the mysteriousness, suggestiveness, and transcendental idealism of his art that have been its greatest legacy to subsequent aesthetic developments.

Footnotes

1
Odilon Redon, Gustave Moreau, Rodolphe Bresdin (New York and Chicago, 1961-1962).

2
French Symbolist Painters (London: Arts Council of Great Britain, 1972).

3
Le Muse Inquietanti, Maestri del Surrealismo (Turin: Galleria Civica d'Arte Moderna, 1967-1968).

4
Odilon Redon . . ., op. cit.

5
Ragnar von Holten, *L'Art Fantastique de Gustave Moreau* (Paris, 1960); expanded in *Gustave Moreau, Symbolist* (Stockholm, 1965).

6
Julius D. Kaplan, *The Art of Gustave Moreau: Theory, Style and Content* (New York: Columbia University, 1972).

7
See the Chronology for Moreau's official recognition.

8
For Moreau as a teacher, see Michel, Rivier, Trapp, Cartier, and Prache in the Bibliography. Also Alfred H. Barr, Jr., *Matisse, His Art and His Public* (New York, 1951), pp. 15-16.

9
Romantic Art in Britain; Paintings and Drawings, 1760-1860 (Detroit and Philadelphia, 1968), esp. pp. 12, 17, 18, 23; Robert Rosenblum, *Transformations in Late Eighteenth Century Art* (Princeton, 1967) suggests this opinion without directly stating it, esp. pp. 3-49; Robert R. Wark, *Ten British Pictures 1740-1840* (San Marino, 1971), esp. pp. 8, 9, 12-13.

10
Gert Schiff, "Die Seltsame Welt des Malers, Gustave Moreau," *Du Atlantis* (Zurich, May 1965), p. 342; Ragnar von Holten, *Gustave Moreau, Symbolist . . ., op. cit.,* pp. 143, 198-199. This assertion would account for many aspects of

Moreau's paintings: the negative role played by women, the svelte, nude male adolescents, and his heroes, whose genitals are often emphasized by the arrangement of the drapery over them. It might also explain his bachelorhood and his loyalty to his mother, with whom he lived and to whom he was devoted until her death.

11
There are numerous portrait drawings of her in the Moreau Museum archive, and one of Moreau's final instructions was to place fresh flowers on her grave on the day of his burial. The design of her tomb is identical to Moreau's, and an engraved initial "A" is superimposed over his initial "G", as a permanent sign of his devotion to her.

12
For complete documentation of this early period, see Pierre-Louis Mathieu, "Documentation inedits sur la jeunesse de Gustave Moreau (1826-1898)," *Bulletin de la Societé de l'Histoire de l'Art Français* (1971), pp. 259-279.

13
Bound volume entitled *Distribution des Prix 1831-1840* at the Collège Rollin in Paris, p. 48. He received this award on August 20, 1839.

14
For a complete discussion of academic training, see Albert Boime, *The Academy and French Painting in the Nineteenth Century* (London, 1971). For this specific reference, see p. 24.

15
Dedreux-Dorcy (1789-1874) had been Géricault's closest friend, and he owned paintings by him that Moreau may have seen. There is no sign, however, of their having influenced Moreau's work of this time.

16
Composizioni di Giovanni Flaxman (Pisa, 1824), pl. XXIII.

17
Mathieu, *op. cit.,* pp. 261, 266-270.

18
This painting is now lost.

19
L'Eclair (Paris, 1852), p. 161.

20
This criticism appeared in an anonymous review that was cut from a newspaper and pasted into a notebook now in the Moreau Museum. The critic was probably comparing Moreau's work with Delacroix's *Pietà* in the Parisian church of Saint-Denis du Saint-Sacrement, 1844.

21
These two materials of painting were believed to represent respectively precision and thus rationalism, and suggestiveness or emotion. This belief was such a truism in the nineteenth century that it could even be caricatured. For example, a cartoonist treating this subject showed Delacroix bearing a brush, jousting with Ingres, who held a pen. (Illustrated in John Rewald, *The History of Impressionism* (New York, 1961), p. 23. For the color-line controversy, see Boime, *op. cit.,* p. 9.

22
Jacques Lethève, *La vie quotidienne des artistes français au XIXe siècle* (Paris, 1968), pp. 53-54, lists Chasseriau's addresses: 1844, 34 rue Frochot; 1847, rue de Laval; in the early 1850s Moreau was living at rue Laval, ave. Frochot 28. (Archives Nationales F21 99)

23
Since the Salon version of *Darius* was repainted in the 1880s (Moreau Museum No. 223), the small oil sketch for it is exhibited here.

24
Edmond Pagnerre, *Journal du Loire;* A. J. du Pays, *Illustration Universelle;* Ch. Tillot, *Journal de Siècle,* June 18, 1853; E. Delecluze, *Journal des Débats.* All in Moreau Museum archives.

25
Henri Peyre, *Bibliographie Critique de l'Héllenisme en France de 1843 à 1870* (New Haven, 1932), esp. pp. 40-48.

26
Magasin Pittoresque (1854), pp. 15-16.

27
Bitumen is a petroleum base used for pigment; it never completely dries and eventually rises to the surface, disintegrating the color.

28
Archives Nationales F21 164. Moreau received 600 francs for the *Pietà* and 2000 francs for *Song of Songs.*

29
Mathieu, *op. cit.,* p. 275.

30
For a discussion of this trip see Barbara Wright, "Gustave Moreau and Eugène Fromentin: a reassessment of their relationship in the light of new documentation," *The Connoisseur,* vol. 180, no. 725 (July 1972), pp. 192-193.

31
Pamela G. Osler, "Gustave Moreau: Some Drawings from the Italian Sojourn," *The National Gallery of Canada Bulletin* (Nov. 1968), pp. 20-26.

32
Some of these were apparently created side by side with Degas. Phoebe Pool, "Degas and Moreau," *The Burlington Magazine,* 105 (June 1963), pp. 251-256, figs. 13, 14.

33
These numbers in parentheses, wherever they appear in this essay, refer to one of the four notebooks of Moreau's writings in the Moreau Museum; the Arabic numeral signifies the specific page. Whenever Moreau dated his note, that information will be recorded, too. The actual quotations are provided in Appendix II of this catalog.

34
Among the dated drawings from nature in the Moreau Museum are *Etampes,* June 19, 1886, No. 1242, Moreau Museum No. 111; *Meréville,* Sept. 17, 1886, No. 1511; *Etampes,* Oct. 14, 1885, No. 1510, and *Honfleur,* Moreau Museum No. 336.

35
See Gilbert Bou, *Gustave Moreau à Decazeville* (Rodez, 1964); Barbara Wright, *op. cit.,* p. 194.

36
See Henri Dorra, "The Guesser Guessed: Gustave Moreau's 'Oedipus'," *Gazette des Beaux-Arts,* 81 (March 1973), pp. 129-140.

37
The Daumier is illustrated in Ragnar von Holten, *Symbolist, op. cit.,* p. 21.

38
The image of the sphinx poised upon Oedipus may derive from Heine's poem "Atta Troll." Von Holten, *Fantastique, op. cit.,* p. 7.

39
Because his mother was deaf, Moreau wrote explanatory notes about his pictures for her.

40
The following discussion is based upon Moreau's note III, 93-94.

41
G. B. de Cavallerii, *Antiquarum Statuarum Urbis Romae* (Rome, 1594).

42
The meaning of this image was explained in the *Magasin Pittoresque* (1834), p. 343, in Moreau's library.

43
This concept first entered the literature in Ary Renan, *Gustave Moreau* (Paris, 1900), pp. 26, 36-42.

44
The whole discussion in this paragraph up to this point is taken from IV, 10, and the manuscript note found among Moreau's loose papers.

45
In the Salon catalog this picture was simply called *Jason*, but a quotation from Ovid (see footnote 47) referred indirectly to Medea. This same catalog contained the dedication of *Young Man and Death* to Chasseriau.

46
Nempe tenens, quod amo, gremioque in Jasonis Haerens Per freta longa ferar: nihil illum amplexa verebor (Ovid, *Metamorphoses*, VIII, 66 ff.).

Translated in *Ovid's Selected Works*, J. C. and M. J. Thornton, eds. (London, 1939), pp. 233-234 (Everyman's Library Series):

As long as I enjoy the thing I love,
And hang about my Jason's neck, it shall
    no whit me move
To sail the dangerous seas; as long as him
I may embrace
Or if I chance to be afraid, my fear shall
    only tend
But for my husband.

47
et auro
Heros Aesonius potitur spolioque superbus
Muneris auctorem secum, spolia altera, portans (Ovid, *Metamorphoses*, VII, 155 ff.).

Translated, as above, p. 238:

Of which his booty being proud, he
    led with him away
The author of his good success, another
    fairer prey.

48
Edith Hamilton, *Mythology* (New York 1942), p. 123.

49
Cat. No. 37, framed with the drawing for *Jason*, does not relate to any specific composition discussed in this catalog, but it is characteristic of the careful preparation that underlies every picture Moreau created.

50
Moreau knew the tradition which used the stories of Ovid to draw moralizing conclusions. He even owned one of these moralized Ovids: *Ovid, Les Métamorphoses* (Paris, 1660).

51
"Une jeune fille recueille pieusement la tête d'Orphée et sa lyre portées par les eaux de l'Hèbre aux rivages de la Thrace."

52
Eug. Droulers (pseudonym for Eugène de Seyn), *Dictionnaire des Attributs, Allegories, Emblémes et Symboles* (Turnhout, 1949), p. 383.

53
Louis Awad, *The Theme of Prometheus in English and French Literature* (Cairo, 1963); Raymond Trousson, *Le Thème de Promethée dans la Littérature Européenne* (Geneva, 1964).

54
Louis Ménard, *Poèmes* (Paris, 1863). My own translation follows:

The golden stars rolling in their
    eternal spheres
Slowly finish their silent rounds.
The incense and murmur of
    plaintive prayers
Have ceased to climb toward the
    tyrant of the skies.
I alone am awake: there is no night or
    dream for me,
And the immortal vulture has no respite
On my torn flanks that are the source of
    my sadness.
For four thousand years his anger
    devours me,
But all that is at last at an end, and
    the dawn
Will light the way for my liberator.

55
Théophile Gautier, *Illustration, Journal Universel*, May 15, 1869. A review by Cl. Bonnin, and an anonymous review in *La France*, May 23, 1869. (All these reviews are pasted into a notebook in the Moreau Museum archive.)

56
Ibid.

57
A. de Pontmartin, *L'Univers Illustré*, May 8, 1869.

58
Charles Clément, *Journal des Débats*, May 14, 1869.

59
Cadars, *op. cit.*, p. 71.

60
Edouard Michel, "Gustave Moreau et ses élèves. Lettres d'Henri Evenepoël à son père," *Mercure de France*, 161 (Jan. 15, 1923), pp. 383-410. Letter of March 10, 1894.

61
Michael Fried, "Manet's Sources: Aspects of His Art, 1859-1865," *Artforum* 7, (March 1969), pp. 28-82. Theodore Reff, "Manet's Sources: a critical evaluation," *Artforum* 8 (Summer 1969), pp. 40-48.

62
Charles Blanc, *Grammaire des Arts du Dessin* ... (Paris, 1867), p. 7.

63
Horace M. Kallen, *Art and Freedom* (New York, 1942), Vol. I, p. 289.

64
The remainder of this paragraph is based upon his notes III, 7, 8.

65
Robert de Montesquiou, Preface to *Exposition Gustave Moreau*, Paris, 1906, p. 7, points out that a specific stylistic relationship between a work of the 1860s and that of the previous decade can be seen in *Diomedus*, Salon of 1866, in which Moreau returned to the portrayal of violent actions characteristic of his work of the 1850s. This is the only major picture to take such a look backwards in stylistic terms.

66
See manuscript note at end of Appendix II.

67
Moreau explained this in a manuscript note in the Moreau Museum that has not been written into the Notebooks.

68
Moreau wrote of these characteristics of
Chateaubriand in a note he did not
inscribe into the notebooks. Now in the
Moreau Museum, it reads,"Chateaubriand
seul y porte son suprême désenchantement,
sa rêverie désesperée de haut vol, et sa
palette idéale — avant tout sa foi de
pélerin.

69
Von Holten, *Fantastique, op. cit.,* p. 19,
suggests the strong influence of
Salammbo on Moreau's *Salome.*

70
Moreau may have influenced Flaubert's
Herodias, written between Nov. 1876
and Feb. 1877, after Moreau's *Salome*
had been highly praised in the Parisian
press.

71
This concept was introduced into the
literature by Ary Renan, *Gustave Moreau,
op. cit.,* pp. 33, 36, 42-44.

72
An early drawing for the figure of Salome
reveals that Moreau was first inspired by
the figure on the far right of Raphael's
Abraham and the Angels in the fourth
bay of the loggia of the Vatican Palace in
Rome.

73
We know this decorative element was
Etruscan because Moreau's source was an
illustration of a piece of Etruscan jewelry
(*Magasin Pittoresque,* 1863, p. 272).

74
Mario Praz, *The Romantic Agony*
(Cleveland and New York, 1956;
originally published 1933).

75
This is documented by a manuscript note
in the Moreau Museum, not inscribed
in the notebooks. It reads: "Je suis obligé
de tout inventer, ne voulant sous aucun
prétexte me servir de toute la vieille
friperie grecque antique."

76
Moreau created an imaginative palace
based on Persian and Moorish architecture
and used Indian, Turkish, Japanese,
Merovingian, and Egyptian ornaments.
One of his sources for such ornamentation
was Owen Jones, *Grammar of Ornament*
(London and Paris, 1865). A copy of
this work was in his library.

77
For example Théodore de Banville sent
him a copy of *Les exiles* (Paris, 1867),
and Heredia's "Jason et Médée," 1872,
was inspired by Moreau's painting of
1865 as cited in Miodrag Ibrovac,
*José-Maria De Heredia, Les Sources
des 'Trophées',* Paris, 1923, p. 13.

78
Moreau's relationship to Naturalism is
explained in the chapter on the Fables of
La Fontaine.

79
Ragnar von Holten, "Gustave Moreau,
Sculpteur," *Revue des Arts,* (Paris)
4-5, 1959, pp. 208-216.

80
Louis Menard, *Du Polythéisme
Hellénique* (Paris, 1863), p. 73. For
Hercules as a solar divinity see Friedrich
Creuzer, "Symbolik und Mythologie der
alten völker…" (1841), 3rd ed., in
Deutsche Schriften (Leipzig and
Darmstadt, 1836-1842), Vol. 2, pp. 610
and note, 614, 628, 655. For the
confusion of Hercules and Apollo
symbolism, *ibid.,* pp. 621, 633.

81
Illustrated in Jacques Thuillier and
Albert Châtelet, *French Painting from
Le Nain to Fragonard* (Geneva, 1964),
p. 243.

82
For example Puvis de Chavannes' *Hope.*
A replica of this picture appeared in the
Salon of 1872 illustrated in Charles
Sterling and Hélène Adhémar *Peintures
Ecole Française, XIXᵉ siècle Musée
Nationale du Louvre* (Paris, 1961),
No. 1528, Plate 592.

83
Of course *Hercules and the Hydra* wasn't
finished until 1876, by which time the
French economy and morale had under-
gone a rapid and spirited rejuvenation.
But, the earlier humiliating defeat still
rankled in every French heart.

84
Jean Paladilhe, *Gustave Moreau,
op. cit.,* p. 37.

85
Preface to *Exposition Gustave Moreau,*
Louvre, 1967.

86
Claudius Grillet, *La Bible dans Victor
Hugo* (Paris, Lyon, 1910), p. 30.*

87
Although this axiom was known to every
great artist, it received special attention
in the nineteenth century. By the 1880s
these theories had been popularized by
Charles Henry and exerted a strong
influence on Seurat. But Moreau gleaned
these same lessons from his study of the
Old Masters. He was aware of this
expressive force and did not subscribe to
the formulas and equations of Henry or
Seurat. Though Moreau differed in style
from many of his contemporaries in the
latter part of the century, the basic
theoretical beliefs were a constant link
among them all.

88
A drawing in the Moreau Museum for
one of the panels is dated 1879. The
panels themselves are dated 1886.

89
Georges Rouault, *Souvenires Intimes*
(Paris, 1927), p. 28.

90
L'Art Moderne (Brussels, July 5, 1881),
p. 111.

91
For example Eliphas Lévi, *Fables et
Symboles* (Paris, 1862), which was in
Moreau's library.

92
The other artists included: J. F.
Jacquemart (1837-1880); Rosa Bonheur
(1822-1899); Paul Baudry (1828-1886);
Gérôme (1824-1904); A. A. E. Hébert
(1870-1908), and Elie Delaunay
(1828-1891).

93
When the Baillehache Collection was
dispersed (sale, Paris, Hôtel Drouot,
May 23, 1922), it included fifty-six
episodes from La Fontaine by thirty-four
artists.

94
For the critical response, see von Holten,
Fantastique, op. cit., p. 38; Georges
Rouault. *ibid.*

95
Photograph available at Bulloz, Paris.

96
Illustrated respectively in Ragnar von
Holten, "Gustave Moreau, Illustrateur
de la Fontaine," *L'Oeil,* 115-116
(July-August, 1964), cover and p. 26;
von Holten, *Fantastique, op. cit.,* pl. 52.

97
Madame Monnier wrote a thesis on the watercolors for the Ecole du Louvre which is unavailable but which she promises to publish in the series "Inventoire des Collections Publiques Françaises"; Jean Paladilhe, *Gustave Moreau* (Paris, 1971).

98
Archives Nationales F²¹ 2142; Jules Guiffrey, "La Manufacture des Gobelins à L'Exhibition de 1900," *L'Exposition de Paris* (1900), 3 vols., I, pp. 268, 270.

99
For one drawing Moreau mentioned that he was using James Burgess' *The Rock-Temples of Elephanta or Ghârâpurî* (London, 1871) as a source.

100
Donald E. Gordon, "On the Origin of the Word 'Expressionism'," *Journal of the Warburg and Courtauld Institutes,* XXIX (1966), pp. 368-369.

101
Dead Lyres is discussed in II, 75-76, written on Dec. 24, 1897.

102
IV, 36.

103
Julius Kaplan, "Gustave Moreau's 'Jupiter and Semele'," *Art Quarterly,* XXXIII, 4 (1970), pp. 393-414.

104
Moreau at this time was studying his copy of *Oeuvres de Flaxman* (Paris, 1836), pl. 24. The figure in question occurs to the far right in *The Torture of Navarios Ciampolo.*

105
Illustrated in von Holten, *Fantastique, op. cit.,* pl. VII.

106
For example, J. Collin de Plancy, *Dictionnaire Infernal* (Paris), in its sixth edition in 1863. He also quoted from Hesiod, Pindar, and Egyptian, Oriental, Phoenician, and Roman mythology.

107
Since both are very similar, only the more complete explanation II, 41, 44, is reprinted in Appendix II.

108
Jules Bois, *Les Petits Religions de Paris* (Paris, 1894), Vol. II, pp. 173-182; Jacques Heugel, *Essai sur la philosophie de Victor Hugo, du point du vue gnostique* (Paris, 1922); Jacques Roos, *Les Idées philosophiques de Victor Hugo* (Paris, 1958), pp. 52, 55, 65, 67, 104.

109
Horace M. Kallen, *Art and Freedom* (New York, 1942), Vol. I, p. 78.

110
Joseph C. Sloan, *Paul Marc Joseph Chenavard* (Chapel Hill, 1962), Robert Pincus-Witten, *Les Salons de la Rose-Croix 1892-1897,* Piccadilly Gallery (London, 1968).

111
Robert Pincus-Witten, *Ibid.,* No. 112.

112
Catalogue Sommaire...du Musée Gustave Moreau, 1926, first page of text.

113
Robert Baldick, "Introduction," Huysmans, *Against Nature* (Baltimore, 1959), pp. 5-14; Paul Jamot, *Maurice Denis* (Paris, 1945), pp. 10-12.

114
J. K. Huysmans, *L'Art Moderne* (Paris, 1883), p. 135.

1.
Copy After Ingres
Pencil on paper
10½ x 4¾ in. (26.7 x 12.0 cm.)
Musée Gustave Moreau, Paris
(1062)

2.
Copy After Rembrandt, 1846
Pencil on paper
6½ x 6¹¹⁄₁₆ in. (16.5 x 17.0 cm.)
Musée Gustave Moreau, Paris
(1063)

1.

2.

3.

3.

Ulysses Recognized by His Nurse
Eurycleia, 1849
Oil on canvas
7½ x 9½ in. (19.0 x 24.2 cm.)
Musée Gustave Moreau, Paris
(15.795)

4.

Drapery Study For Ulysses Recognized by
His Nurse Eurycleia, 1849
Pencil, charcoal, white chalk on tan paper
8⅜ x 9½ in. (21.3 x 24.1 cm.)
Musée Gustave Moreau, Paris

4.

5.
Study of The Nurse For Ulysses
Recognized by His Nurse Eurycleia, 1849
Pencil, charcoal, white chalk on tan paper
12 x 7 in. (30.5 x 17.8 cm.)
Musée Gustave Moreau, Paris
6.
Pieta, 1852
Etching
7⅛ x 9⅛ in. (18.1 x 23.2 cm.)
Musée Gustave Moreau, Paris
(archive)

5.

6.

7.
Horseman, ca. 1853
Oil on canvas
15 x 18⅛ in. (38.0 x 46.0 cm.)
Musée Gustave Moreau, Paris
(632)

8.
Hamlet Poisoning The King,
ca. 1852-1854
Pencil, pen and ink on paper
11⅞ x 9⅞ in. (30.2 x 25.3 cm.)
Musée Gustave Moreau, Paris
(archive)

7.

8.

9.
Darius Fleeing After The Battle of
Arbela Stops Exhausted To Drink In A
Pond, 1853
Oil on canvas
10⅝ x 6⁵⁄₁₆ in. (27.0 x 16.0 cm.)
Musée Gustave Moreau, Paris
(604)
10.
The Herald
Watercolor on paper
5⁵⁄₁₆ x 6⁵⁄₁₆ in. (15.0 x 16.0 cm.)
Musée Gustave Moreau, Paris
(310)

9.

10.

*The Athenians Delivered To The
Minotaur In The Labyrinth On Crete,*
1855
Oil on canvas
42 x 79 in. (106.0 x 200.0 cm.)
Musée de L'Ain, Bourg-en-Bresse
◄

12.
*Study For The Athenians Delivered
To The Minotaur,* ca. 1855
Pencil, pen, brush, brown ink and wash,
white watercolor on paper
9⅛ x 5⅞ in. (23.2 x 14.9 cm.)
Musée Gustave Moreau, Paris
(357)

13.
*Study For The Athenians Delivered
To The Minotaur,* ca. 1855
Pencil, pen, brush, brown ink and wash,
white watercolor on paper
9⅛ x 5⅞ in. (23.2 x 14.9 cm.)
Musée Gustave Moreau, Paris
(357)
14.
*Study For Hercules In Hercules And The
Daughters Of Thestius,* ca. 1852-1854
Red chalk on paper
16½ x 11⅜ in. (42.0 x 29.0 cm.)
Musée Gustave Moreau, Paris
(2135)

13.

14.

15.
Study For Young Man And Death,
ca. 1865
Oil on canvas
11 x 7^{11}⁄$_{16}$ in. (28.0 x 20.0 cm.)
Musée Gustave Moreau, Paris
(642)

15.

16.

Statuette Of Apollo, 1859
Pencil and watercolor on paper
9⅞ x 3¹¹⁄₁₆ in. (25.0 x 9.3 cm.)
Musée Gustave Moreau, Paris
(28)

16.

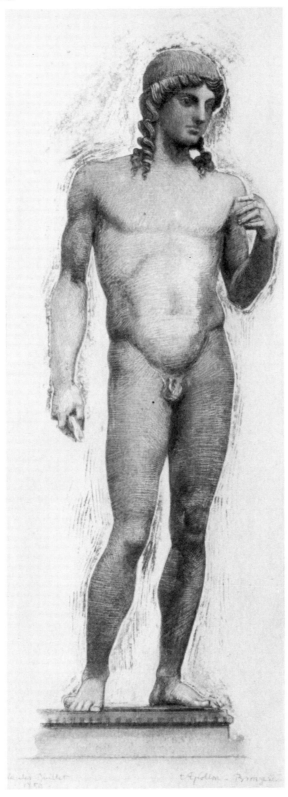

17.
Copy After Raphael, 1858
Oil on canvas
15⁹⁄₁₆ x 10 in. (39.5 x 26.0 cm.)
Musée Gustave Moreau, Paris
(13636)
18.
Copy After Michelangelo's Sistine Chapel
Watercolor, pen, black and red ink
on paper
22 x 16¾ in. (56.0 x 42.0 cm.)
Musée Gustave Moreau, Paris
(salle C, Ser. 11-1-19)

18.

19.
*Copy After Titian's Adoration Of
The Magi,* 1858
Watercolor on paper
10 x 20¼ in. (25.4 x 51.4 cm.)
Musée Gustave Moreau, Paris
(13647)
20.
Hesiod And The Muse, 1857
Pencil, pen and brown ink on paper
16½ x 13 in. (42.0 x 33.0 cm.)
Mr. Germain Seligman, New York

19.

20.

21.
Academie, ca. 1858
Pencil and charcoal on paper
14⅛ x 6⅜ in. (33.2 x 16.2 cm.)
Musée Gustave Moreau, Paris
(718)

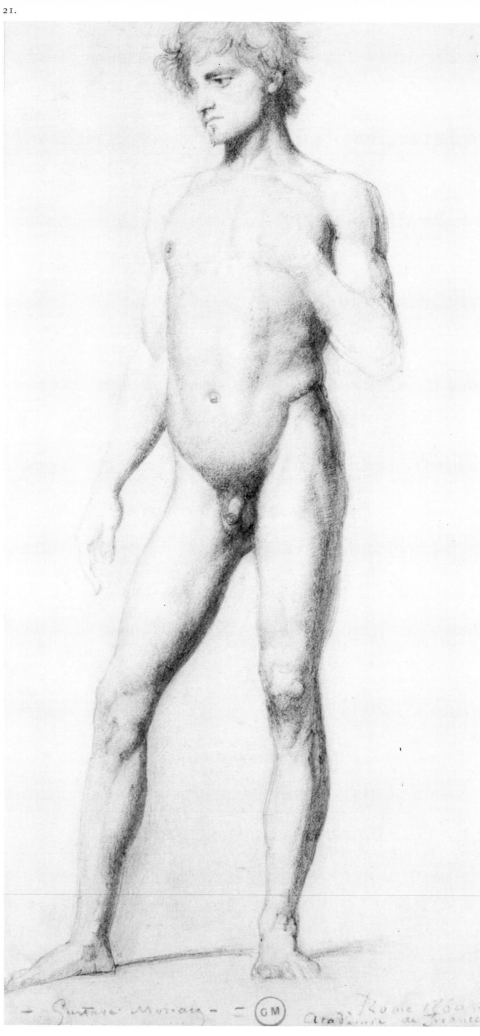

22.

*Studies From The Nude And An
Academie,* 1858
8¼ x 10⅝ in. (21.0 x 27.0 cm.)
Musée Gustave Moreau, Paris
(719)

22.

23.
Italian Coast, 1859
Pencil, charcoal and watercolor on
grey-green paper
6¼ x 8⅝ in. (16.0 x 22.0 cm.)
Musée Gustave Moreau, Paris
(377)
24.
Roman Landscape, 1858
Pastel on paper
6⁵⁄₁₆ x 9¹⁄₁₆ in. (16.0 x 23.0 cm.)
Musée Gustave Moreau, Paris
(459)

23.

24.

25.
Autumnal Landscape
Charcoal and watercolor on paper
5⅞ x 9¹⁄₁₆ in. (15.0 x 23.0 cm.)
Musée Gustave Moreau, Paris
(328)

25.

26.
Landscape, Etampes, ca. 1885-1886
Charcoal and watercolor on paper
6⅝₁₆ x 4⅝₁₆ in. (16.0 x 11.0 cm.)
Musée Gustave Moreau, Paris
(465)

27.
Italian Peasant, Seen From The Back,
ca. 1857-59
Watercolor on white paper
7½ x 3⅛ in. (19.0 x 8.0 cm.)
Musée Gustave Moreau, Paris
(479)

27.

28.

Oedipus And The Sphinx, 1864
Oil on canvas
81¼ x 41¼ in. (206.4 x 104.7 cm.)
The Metropolitan Museum of Art,
New York

28.

First Idea For Oedipus And The Sphinx,
1861
Pencil, pen and ink on paper
11⅛ x 5⅝ in. (29.0 x 14.0 cm.)
Musée Gustave Moreau, Paris
(517)

30.
Study For Oedipus In De Cavaleriis,
Antiquarum Statuarum Urbis Romae,
ca. 1860
Pencil on paper
Musée Gustave Moreau, Paris
(14629)
31.
Oedipus And The Sphinx, ca. 1860
Watercolor on paper
12⁹⁄₁₆ x 8⅝ in. (32.0 x 22.0 cm.)
Musée Gustave Moreau, Paris
(569)

30.

31.

32.
Study For Oedipus
Pencil on paper
10¾ x 9 in. (27.8 x 22.8 cm.)
Musée Gustave Moreau, Paris
(2840)

33.
Study For The Sphinx's Wing In Oedipus
Pencil on paper
11¹³⁄₁₆ x 7⅝ in. (29.9 x 19.4 cm.)
Musée Gustave Moreau, Paris
(2489)

32.

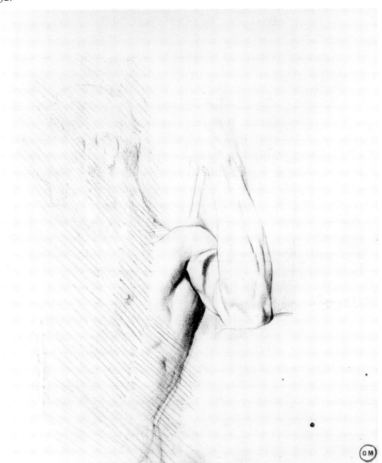

33.

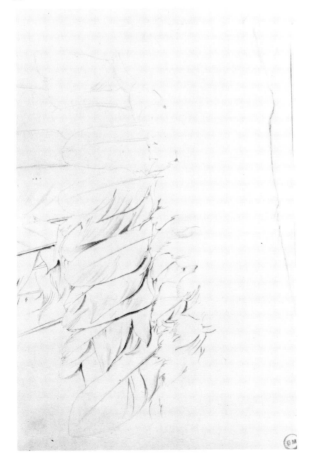

34.
Jason And Medea, ca. 1865
Pencil, pen and ink on paper
7¹¹⁄₁₆ x 4⅛ in. (19.5 x 10.4 cm.)
Musée Gustave Moreau, Paris
(1754)

34.

35.
Jason, ca. 1865
Pencil on paper
7½ x 4⁵⁄₁₆ in. (19.0 x 11.0 cm.)
Musée Gustave Moreau, Paris
(1755)

36.

Study For Jason, ca. 1865
Red and white chalk on grey paper
16¼ x 8⅞ in. (41.3 x 22.5 cm.)
Musée Gustave Moreau, Paris
(1973)

36.

37.
Drapery Study
Pencil and white chalk on
grey-brown paper
6$\frac{5}{16}$ x 10$\frac{7}{8}$ in. (16.0 x 27.7 cm.)
Musée Gustave Moreau, Paris
(1974)

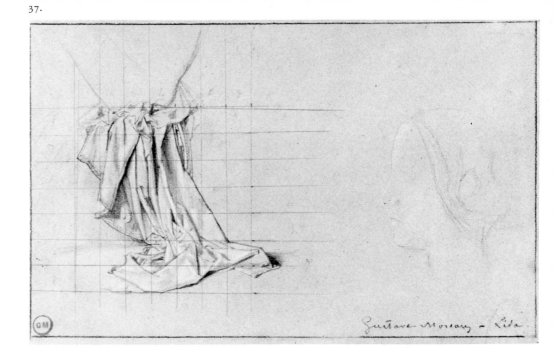

38.
Orpheus, ca. 1865
Oil on canvas
39½ x 25½ in. (100.5 x 64.8 cm.)
Washington University, St. Louis

39.
Orpheus, ca. 1866
Pencil on paper
10 1/16 x 6 5/8 in. (25.5 x 17.0 cm.)
Musée Gustave Moreau, Paris
(2894)

40.
The Saint And The Poet, 1868
Watercolor on paper
11⅜ x 6½ in. (28.9 x 16.5 cm.)
Picadilly Gallery, London
41.
Prometheus, 1868
Oil on canvas
80 x 48⅝ in. (205.0 x 122.0 cm.)
Musée Gustave Moreau, Paris
(196)

40.

GVSTAVE MOREAV : 1868 ·   PROMETHEVS ·

42.

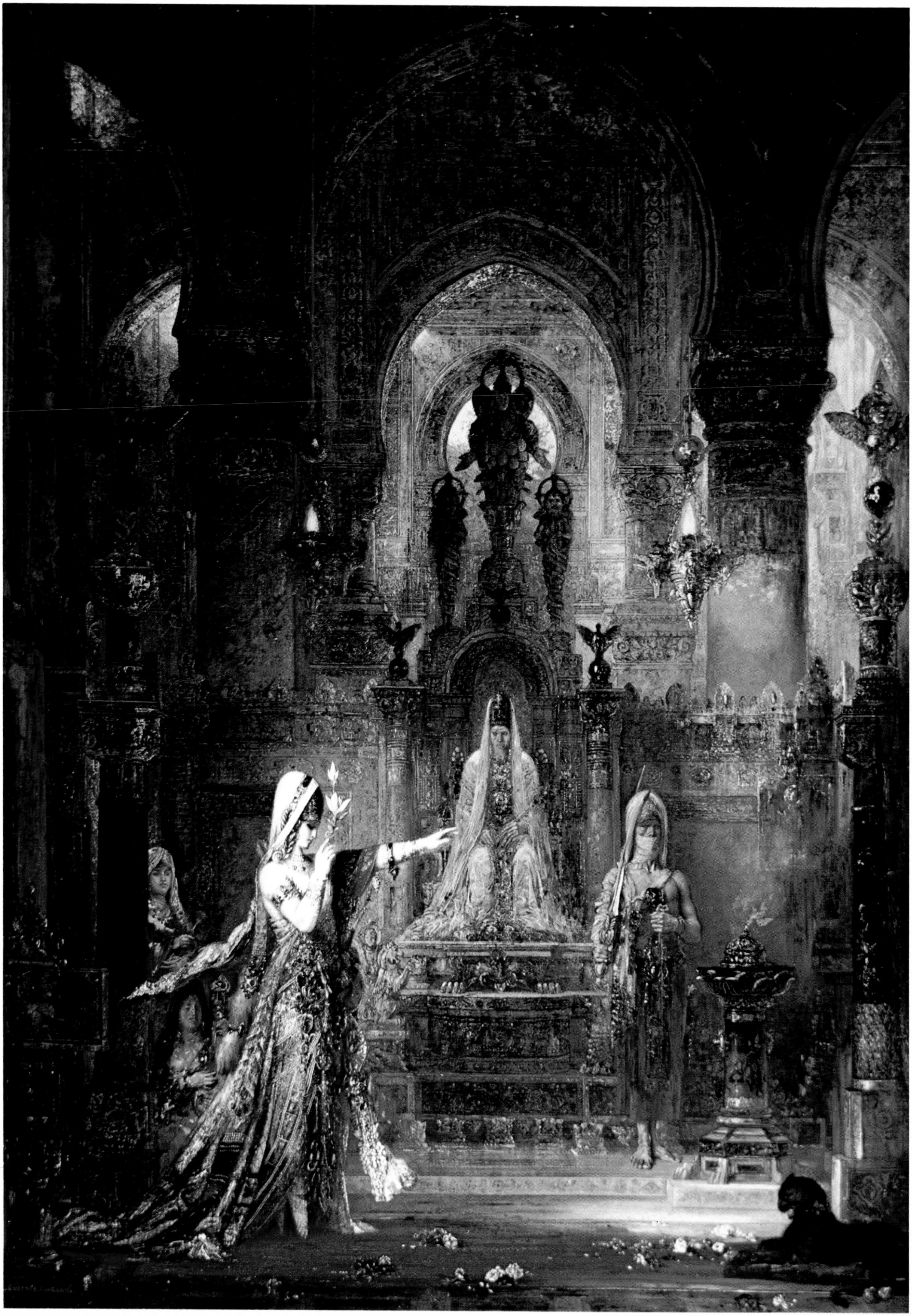

42.
Salome Dancing Before Herod, 1876
Oil on canvas
56⅝ x 41¹/₁₆ in. (143.8 x 104.2 cm.)
The Armand Hammer Collection,
Los Angeles

43.
*Study For Herodias In Salome Dancing
Before Herod,* ca. 1872-1875
Pencil on tracing paper
13⅝ x 3¹⁵/₁₆ in. (34.9 x 9.9 cm.)
Musée Gustave Moreau, Paris
(2274)

43.

44.

44.
*Study For Herod In Salome Dancing
Before Herod,* ca. 1872-1875
Pencil, pen and ink on tracing paper
13¹¹⁄₁₆ x 10⅜ in. (34.9 x 26.3 cm.)
Musée Gustave Moreau, Paris
(2275)

45.
*Study For Salome In Salome Dancing
Before Herod,* ca. 1872-1875
Pencil, pen and ink on tracing paper
18 x 8⅝ in. (45.8 x 21.8 cm.)
Musée Gustave Moreau, Paris
(2276)

45.

46.
*Study For The Executioner In Salome
Dancing Before Herod,* ca. 1872-1875
Pencil on tracing paper
17 x 6¹¹⁄₁₆ in. (43.2 x 15.8 cm.)
Musée Gustave Moreau, Paris
(2277)
47.
Study For Salome Dancing Before Herod,
ca. 1872-1875
Oil on panel
12⅝ x 9⅞ in. (32.0 x 25.0 cm.)
Musée Gustave Moreau, Paris
(751)

46.

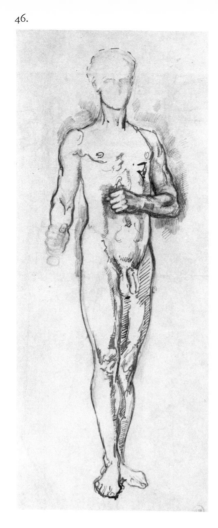

47.

48.
Study For Salome Dancing Before Herod,
ca. 1872-1875
Pencil on paper
9 x 10⁹⁄₁₆ in. (22.8 x 26.8 cm.)
Musée Gustave Moreau, Paris
(2307)
49.
Salome
Pencil and charcoal on paper
23⁴⁄₁₆ x 13⁹⁄₁₆ in. (59.0 x 34.5 cm.)
Musée Gustave Moreau, Paris
(25) (13966)

48.

49.

50.
Hercules And The Hydra Of Lerna, 1876
Oil on canvas
69 x 60½ in. (175.3 x 153.5 cm.)
Art Institute of Chicago

51.
Apollo And Python
Oil on panel
9 x 6 in. (23.0 x 15.3 cm.)
National Gallery of Canada, Ottawa

51.

52.
*Study For Hercules And The Hydra
Of Lerna,* ca. 1869-1875
Charcoal on buff paper
7¹³⁄₁₆ x 6 in. (19.8 x 15.2 cm.)
Musée Gustave Moreau, Paris
(2097)

52.

53.
*Study For Hercules And The Hydra
Of Lerna,* ca. 1869-1875
Pencil on paper
3¾ x 4¾ in. (9.5 x 12.0 cm.)
Musée Gustave Moreau, Paris
(2098)
54.
*Study For Hercules And The Hydra
Of Lerna,* ca. 1869-1875
Pencil on white paper
3⁹⁄₁₆ x 3¹⁵⁄₁₆ in. (9.0 x 10.0 cm.)
Musée Gustave Moreau, Paris
(2099)

53.

54.

55.
Calvary, 1867
Oil on canvas
9⁷⁄₁₆ x 12⁹⁄₁₆ in. (24.0 x 32.0 cm.)
Musée du Louvre, Paris
56.
St. Sebastian, ca. 1878
Pencil, charcoal and sanguine on paper
24³⁄₁₆ x 14¹⁄₁₆ in. (61.5 x 35.8 cm.)
Musée Gustave Moreau, Paris
(827)

55.

56.

57.
Jacob And The Angel, ca. 1878
Watercolor on paper
7³⁄₁₆ x 4 in. (18.5 x 10.0 cm.)
Musée Gustave Moreau, Paris
(13988)

57.

58.
David, ca. 1878
Oil on canvas
38$\frac{15}{16}$ x 21$\frac{1}{4}$ in. (98.0 x 54.0 cm.)
Musée Gustave Moreau, Paris
(199)

58.

59.
Saint Cecilia
Pen, ink and oil on panel
19¹¹⁄₁₆ x 13¾ in. (50.0 x 35.0 cm.)
Musée Gustave Moreau, Paris
(754)

60.

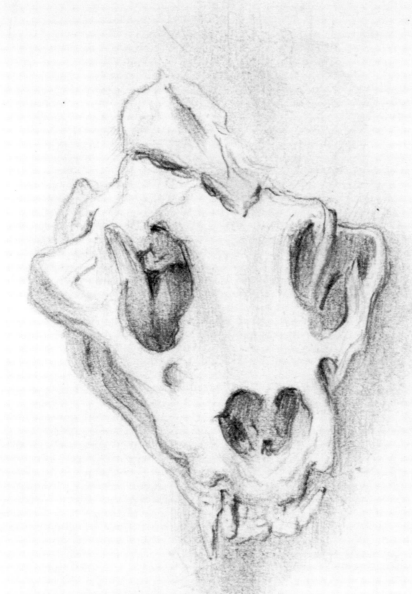

Lion de Barbarie

Jardin des Plantes

Galeries d'anatomie Comparée

- 10 Septembre - 1881 - - Gustave Moreau -

GM

60.
Study Of Animal Skull, 1881
Pencil on paper
7¹³⁄₁₆ x 5½ in. (19.8 x 14.0 cm.)
Musée Gustave Moreau, Paris
(1274)
61.
Study Of Animal Skull, ca. 1879-1886
Pencil on white paper
7 x 10⅝ in. (17.8 x 27.0 cm.)
Musée Gustave Moreau, Paris
(1275)
62.
Study Of Animal Skull, ca. 1879-1886
Red and lead pencil, charcoal on
cream paper
7¹³⁄₁₆ x 13¾ in. (19.8 x 35.0 cm.)
Musée Gustave Moreau, Paris
(1276)

61.

62.

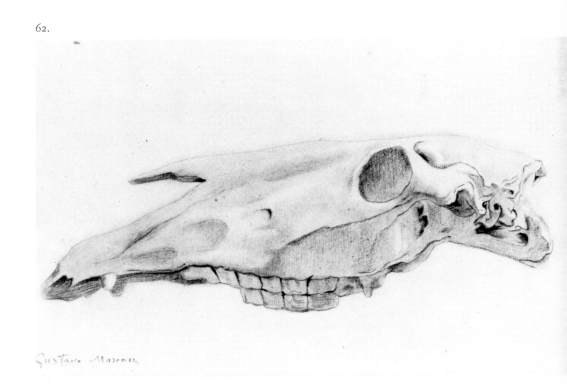

63.
Phoebus And Boreas, ca. 1879
Watercolor
11⅜ x 8¼ in. (29.0 x 21.0 cm.)
Musée Gustave Moreau, Paris
(492)

63.

64.
Study For A Figure In Hercules
And The Daughters Of Thestius, 1883
Pencil on white paper
13⅜ x 7½ in. (34.0 x 19.0 cm.)
Musée Gustave Moreau, Paris
(2233)

64.

65.
The Dragon With Many Heads And
The Dragon With Many Tails,
ca. 1879-1881
Pencil on buff paper
11 x 8⁷⁄₁₆ in. (28.0 x 21.5 cm.)
Musée Gustave Moreau, Paris
(2607)
66.
The Lion And The Gnat, ca. 1879-1881
Black ink wash on blue paper
Musée Gustave Moreau, Paris
(2605)

65.

66.

67.
The Mogul's Dream, ca. 1879-1881
Pencil, pen and ink on tracing paper
10⅜ x 8 in. (26.4 x 20.2 cm.)
Musée Gustave Moreau, Paris
(2606)
68.
The Monkey And The Leopard,
ca. 1881-1886
Pencil on paper
Musée Gustave Moreau, Paris
(2608)

67.

68.

Gustave Moreau.

69.
The Peacock Complaining To Juno,
ca. 1881-86
Watercolor
11 ⅜ x 7 ½ in. (29.0 x 19.0 cm.)
Musée Gustave Moreau, Paris
(566 bis)
70.
The Wolf And The Lamb, ca. 1881-86
Pencil and watercolor on paper
11 x 7 ½ in. (28.0 x 19.0 cm.)
Musée Gustave Moreau, Paris
(300)

70.

71.
The Frogs Asked For A King,
ca. 1881-86
$12\frac{3}{16}$ x $7\frac{7}{8}$ in. (31.0 x 20.0 cm.)
Musée Gustave Moreau, Paris
(448)

72.
Hercules And The Doe
Watercolor on paper
8¾ x 6 in. (22.0 x 14.0 cm.)
Musée Gustave Moreau, Paris
(320)

73.
Dante And Virgil
Watercolor
6⅝₁₆ x 9¹³⁄₁₆ in. (16.0 x 25.0 cm.)
Musée Gustave Moreau, Paris
(470)
74.
The Prodigal Son
Watercolor
4¾ x 11⁷⁄₁₆ in. (12.0 x 29.0 cm.)
Musée Gustave Moreau, Paris
(417)
75.
Centaurs Carrying A Dead Poet
Watercolor
14⁵⁄₁₆ x 9⁷⁄₁₆ in. (11.0 x 24.0 cm.)
Musée Gustave Moreau, Paris
(484)

73.

74.

75.

76.
The Siren And The Poet, 1896-99
Tapestry
137½ x 94½ in. (351.0 x 241.0 cm.)
Mobilier Nationale, Paris
77.
The Triumph Of Alexander The Great,
ca. 1890
Oil, watercolor, tempera on canvas
61 x 61 in. (155.0 x 155.0 cm.)
Musée Gustave Moreau, Paris
(70)
78.
Detail For The Triumph Of Alexander
Pencil, brush and ink on tracing paper
14¹⁄₁₆ x 17¾ in. (35.8 x 45.0 cm.)
Musée Gustave Moreau, Paris
(3096)

77.

78.

79.
Orestes And The Erynnies, 1891
Oil on canvas
70 x 48½ in. (180.0 x 120.0 cm.)
Giovanni Agnelli, Turin
(not in exhibition)
80.
Oil Sketch
Oil on panel
14⁹⁄₁₆ x 18⁵⁄₁₆ in. (37.0 x 46.5 cm.)
Musée Gustave Moreau, Paris
(1135)
81.
Oil Sketch
Oil on panel
9⁹⁄₁₆ x 8⅝ in. (24.3 x 21.9 cm.)
Musée Gustave Moreau, Paris
(1153)

79.

80.

82.

82.
Oil Sketch
Oil on wood
12⁹⁄₁₆ x 15¾ in. (32.0 x 40.0 cm.)
Musée Gustave Moreau, Paris
(1140)
83.
The Good Samaritan
Oil on canvas
28⁵⁄₁₆ x 39⅜ in. (82.0 x 100.0 cm.)
Musée Gustave Moreau, Paris
(78)

83.

84.

The Ideal Flower—The Catholic Church,
ca. 1890-1898
Charcoal and watercolor
13¾ x 9⁷⁄₁₆ in. (35.0 x 24.0 cm.)
Musée Gustave Moreau, Paris
(974)

85.

St. John Of The Apocalypse, 1896
Pencil and watercolor on white paper
4¾ x 3⅝ in. (12.0 x 9.3 cm.)
Musée Gustave Moreau, Paris
(843)

84.

85.

86.
Argonauts, ca. 1897
Watercolor
13¼ x 8⅝ in. (33.7 x 22.0 cm.)
Musée Gustave Moreau, Paris
(844)
87.
Jupiter And Semele, 1889
Oil on canvas
31½ x 21⅝ in. (80.0 x 55.0 cm.)
Musée Gustave Moreau, Paris
(94)
88.
*Study For Bacchus And Semele For
Jupiter And Semele,* ca. 1890
Pencil on paper
16¾ x 11¹¹⁄₁₆ in. (42.5 x 29.7 cm.)
Musée Gustave Moreau, Paris
(1580)

86.

87.

88.

Sémélé

Gustave Moreau

The Catalog

Musée Gustave Moreau, Paris; No. refers to the published catalog.

Musée Gustave Moreau, Paris; Drawings No. refers to the numbers that have recently been assigned to the exhibited drawings in the Museum.

Musée Gustave Moreau, Paris; Inventory No. refers to the inventory which catalogs all the works in the Museum even when they are not on exhibition and not in the published catalogs.

Musée Gustave Moreau, Paris; Archives refers to the loose drawings and notebooks that are kept in the Salle de Conference and storerooms of the Museum.

1.
Copy after Ingres
Pencil on paper
10½ x 4¾ in. (26.7 x 12.0 cm.)
Inscribed and signed upper right:
Madame . . . d'apres J. A. Ingres/
Rome 1817/Gustave Moreau

Collection:
Musée Gustave Moreau, Paris;
Drawings No. 1062

Literature:
For the original drawings by Ingres
see Daniel Ternois, *Les Dessins d'Ingres
au Musée de Montauban. Les Portraits,*
Vol. III of Inventaire Général des Dessins
des Musées de Province, Paris, 1959.
No. 97.

2.
Copy after Rembrandt, 1846
Pencil on paper
6½ x 6¹¹⁄₁₆ in. (16.5 x 17.0 cm.)
Inscribed, signed, and dated lower left:
D'apres Rembrandt
Gustave Moreau/1846

Collection:
Musée Gustave Moreau, Paris;
Drawings No. 1063

3.
*Ulysses Recognized by His Nurse,
Eurycleia,* 1849
Oil on canvas
7½ x 9½ in. (19.0 x 24.2 cm.)
Inscribed lower left: Esquisse de la
Nourrice d'Ulysse

Collection:
Musée Gustave Moreau, Paris;
Inventory No. 15795

Literature:
For the finished painting, Lord Pilgrim,
"Mouvement des Arts . . . Les concours
por l'ecole de Rome," *L'Artiste,* Paris.
Vᵉ série, Tome III, Oct. 1, 1849,
pp. 207-208.

4.
*Drapery Study for Ulysses Recognized by
His Nurse, Eurycleia,* 1849
Pencil, charcoal, white chalk on tan paper
8⅜ x 9½ in. (21.3 x 24.1 cm.)
Signed and inscribed upper left:
Gustave Moreau — (Loges)

Collection:
Musée Gustave Moreau, Paris;
Drawings No. 3943

5.
*Study of the Nurse for Ulysses
Recognized by His Nurse, Eurycleia,* 1849
Charcoal on beige paper touched in
white chalk
12 x 7 in. (30.5 x 17.8 cm.)
Inscribed upper left: En loge —
Beaux Arts/Concour de l'Ulysse
Signed and dated upper right:
Gustave Moreau/1849

Collection:
Musée Gustave Moreau, Paris;
Drawings No. 3944

Literature:
Mathieu, 1971, p. 265

6.
Pietà, 1852
Etching
7⅛ x 9⅛ in. (18.1 x 23.2 cm.)
Dated and initialed lower middle
(in reverse) 1852 GM

Collection:
Musée Gustave Moreau, Paris; Archives

Literature:
Mathieu, 1971, pp. 268, 279 (fig. 2)
Paladilhe, 1971, p. 11

7.
Horseman, ca. 1853
Oil on canvas
15 x 18⅛ in. (38.0 x 46.0 cm.)

Collection:
Musée Gustave Moreau, Paris; No. 632

Literature:
Cadars, 1965, p. 40

8.
Hamlet Poisoning the King,
ca. 1852-1854
Pencil, pen and ink on paper
11⅞ x 9⅞ in. (30.2 x 25.3 cm.)
Signed and inscribed lower right:
Gustave Moreau — Hamlet

Collection:
Musée Gustave Moreau, Paris; Archives

Literature:
Cadars, 1965, pp. 40-41
Mathieu, 1971, pp. 277-279 (fig. 4)
Although dated 1854 by Mathieu, recent
research in Moreau's early sketchbooks
by Gerhard Fries reveals that Moreau was
working in this style as early as 1852.
When Moreau decided to have some
drawings engraved, he may well have
chosen something that had been
completed earlier. I am grateful to
Mr. Fries for sharing with me the results
of his research, still in progress, which
promises to clarify and revise the
chronology of Moreau's early work.

9.
Darius, Fleeing after the Battle of Arbela, Stops Exhausted to Drink in a Pond, 1853
Oil on canvas
10⅝ x 6$\frac{5}{16}$ in. (27.0 x 16.0 cm.)
Initialed lower left: GM

Collection:
Musée Gustave Moreau, Paris; No. 604

Literature:
For the finished painting
Chesneau, 1868, p. 181
Leprieur, 1889, p. 10
Flat, 1889, p. 12, unnumbered plate
Renan, 1900, p. 132
1906 – Paris, p. 7
Pool, 1971, pp. 11, 83

10.
The Herald
Watercolor on paper
5$\frac{15}{16}$ x 6$\frac{5}{16}$ in. (15.0 x 16.0 cm.)
Signed lower right: Gustave Moreau

Collection:
Musée Gustave Moreau; No. 310

11.
The Athenians Delivered to the Minotaur in the Labyrinth on Crete, 1855
Oil on canvas
42 x 79 in. (106.0 x 200.0 cm.)

Collection:
Musée de l'Ain, Bourg-en-Bresse

Exhibitions:
Salon of 1855 (Universal Exhibition), No. 3703
Bourg-en-Bresse, Musée de l'Ain, *Le Centenaire du Musée,* 1954, No. 122
Ambérieu-en-Bugey, Château des Allymes, *Un demi-siècle de vie poétique à travers Gabriel-Vicaire,* May 24-Sept. 30, 1969, No. 219
Paris, Musée des Arts Decoratifs, *"Equivoques" Peintures française du XIXe Siècle,* March 9-May 14, 1973, (illus.)

Literature:
Maxime Du Camp, "Salon de 1864," *Revue des Deux Mondes,* 1864, p. 705
Leprieur, 1889, p. 10
Renan, 1900, p. 132
Anonymous, 1914, p. 28
Focillon, 1928, p. 88
Cadars, 1965, p. 44
Mathieu, 1971, pp. 269-270
Paladilhe, 1971, p. 12
Dorra, 1973, pp. 129, 131 (fig. 2)

12.
Study for the Athenians Delivered to the Minotaur, ca. 1855
Pencil, pen, brush, brown ink and wash, white watercolor on paper
9⅛ x 5⅞ in. (23.2 x 14.9 cm.)

Collection:
Musée Gustave Moreau, Paris; No. 357

13.
Study for the Athenians Delivered to the Minotaur, ca. 1855
Pen, brush, brown ink and wash, white watercolor on paper
9⅛ x 5⅞ in. (23.2 x 14.9 cm.)

Collection:
Musée Gustave Moreau, Paris; No. 357

14.
Study for Hercules in Hercules and the Daughters of Thestius, ca. 1852-1854
Red chalk on paper
16½ x 11⅜ in. (42.0 x 29.0 cm.)
Signed lower left: Gustave Moreau
Inscribed lower right: Filles de Thestius

Collection:
Musée Gustave Moreau, Paris;
Drawings No. 2185

Literature:
For the large oil painting
Notebook II 57, 58, 92; III 45; IV 48, 49
Flat, 1899, p. 13
Musée Gustave Moreau, 1904, p. 7
(illus. between pp. 50 and 51)
Dreyfus, 1914, p. 172
von Holten, 1960, pp. 23-24
(repr. fig. 30)
Pool, 1963, p. 255
Biehler, 1964, pp. 78-79
Schiff, 1965, pp. 342, 359
(illus. pp. 348-349)
von Holten, 1965, pp. 61-63
(illus. p. 62)
Paladilhe, 1971, pp. 12, 64, 118, 123
(illus. No. 75)
Mathieu, 1974, pp. 33, 73
(illus. pp. 28, 29)
Hercules and the Daughters of Thestius has always been dated 1852 because of the chronology of Moreau's work that Henry Rupp wrote in a notebook in the Moreau Museum, probably in the 1890s. In fact, a precise date is untenable at this stage of research on Moreau. The stylistic similarity between drawings for this work and for *The Athenians* which appear in the same sketchbooks requires a broader date until further research clarifies this problem. I owe this information to Gerhard Fries (see note for cat. no. 8).

15.
Study for Young Man and Death, ca. 1865
Oil on canvas
11 x 7$\frac{11}{16}$ in. (28.0 x 20.0 cm.)

Collection:
Musée Gustave Moreau, Paris; No. 642

Literature:
For studies of this work
Wright, 1972, p. 195
For the large finished oil
C. Blanc, *L'Avenir National,* June 3, 1865
A. de Bullement, *Les Beaux-Arts,* May 15, 1865
E. Chesneau, *Le Constitutionnel,* May 9, 1865
C. Clément, *Journal des Débats,* May 10, 1865
T. Gautier, *Le Moniteur Universel,* July 9, 1865
M. de Montifaud, *L'Artiste,* May 15, 1865
C. de Mouy, *Revue Française,* June 1, 1865
Revue des Deux Mondes, June 1, 1865, pp. 663-665
De Sault, *Le Temps,* May 24, 1865
Thilda, *La Vie Parisienne,* May 6, 1865 and May 13, 1865 (caricature)
J. Walter, *L'Entracte,* May 17, 1865
C. Blanc, *Le Temps,* Aug. 27, 1867
(reprinted in *Les Artistes de mon temps, Paris,* 1876, pp. 468-469)
E. Chesneau, *Le Constitutionnel,* Sept. 10, 1867
E. Chesneau, 1868, pp. 192-193
C. Blanc, *Les artistes de mon temps,* Paris, 1876, pp. 468-469
Leprieur, 1889, p. 41
White, 1897, p. 4
Flat, 1899, pp. 10-11
Schuré, 1904, pp. 364-365
Laran, 1913, pp. 31-32
Anonymous, 1914, pp. 39-40
Coquiot, 1924, p. 110
Proust, 1958, p. 308
von Holten, 1960, pp. 10-11
Biehler, 1964, pp. 64-65
Schiff, 1965, p. 359
von Holten, 1965, pp. 31-32, 197
(illus. p. 32)
Paladilhe, 1971, pp. 13, 26, 92, 113
Dorra, 1973, pp. 130-131
Frongia, 1973 (fig. 2a)

16.
Statuette of Apollo, 1859
Pencil and watercolor on paper
9⅞ x 3$\frac{11}{16}$ in. (25.0 x 9.3 cm.)
Inscribed lower left: Naples Juillet 1859
Inscribed lower right: Apollon Bronzes

Collection:
Musée Gustave Moreau, Paris; Inventory No. 13636

Literature:
For a general discussion of his copies in Naples
Paladilhe, 1971, p. 19

17.
Copy after Raphael's, Portrait of a Man, 1858
Oil on canvas
15$\frac{9}{16}$ x 10 in. (39.5 x 26.0 cm.)
Inscribed, signed, and dated lower left:
d'après Holbein – Gustave Moreau/
Galerie Borghèse – Florence – 1858

Collection:
Musée Gustave Moreau, Paris; Inventory
No. 18

Moreau's copy is a slight reduction from
the original picture which is still in
the Borghese Gallery (17 11/16 x 11 7/8 in.;
45.0 x 30.0 cm.). When Moreau copied
this picture, it was believed to be by
Holbéin. See Paolo Della Pergola,
Galleria Borghese I Dipinti, Rome, 1959,
Vol. II, No. 168, pp. 113-114.

18.
Copy after Michelangelo's Sistine Chapel
Watercolor, pen, black and red ink
on paper
22 x 16¾ in. (56.0 x 42.5 cm.)

Collection:
Musée Gustave Moreau, Paris; Salle C,
Meuble 1, Série 2, premier panneau, recto

Literature:
Paladilhe, 1971, p. 14
For a general reference to Michelangelo
Restany, 1964, p. 84

19.
*Copy after Titian's Adoration of the
Magi*, 1858
Watercolor on paper
10 x 20¼ in. (25.4 x 51.4 cm.)
Inscribed lower left: Milan Août 1858
d'après Titien
Moreau copied the original oil
(118 x 222 cm.) in the Ambrosiana in
Milan; see Francesco Valconover,
Tutta La Pittura di Tiziano, Milan, 1960,
vol. II, p. 42, pl. 77.

Collection:
Musée Gustave Moreau, Paris; Inventory
No. 13647

Literature:
For a general mention of Venetian art
Paladilhe, 1971, p. 17
For a general mention of his love for
Titian
Loisel, 1912, p. 31
Rouault, 1946-1947, p. 62

20.
Hesiod and the Muse, 1857
Pencil, pen and brown ink on paper
16½ x 13 in. (42.0 x 33.0 cm.)
Signed, dated, and inscribed lower right:
Gustave Moreau 1857 Rome
Inscribed upper left: Hesiode et la Muse

Collections:
Madame Alexandre Singer (given to
Emile Olivier)
Mr. and Mrs. Germain Seligman,
New York

Exhibitions:
Paris, 1906, No. 193
New York, Jacques Seligmann & Co., Inc.
Master Drawings, Nov. 7-28, 1960,
No. 26
Dayton, Dayton Art Institute, *French*

Artists in Italy, 1600-1900, Oct. 15-
Nov. 28, 1971, No. 49 (illus. p. 28)

Literature:
Osler, 1968, pp. 22, 26 (illus. p. 25)

21.
Académie, ca. 1858
Pencil and charcoal on paper
14⅛ x 6⅜ in. (33.2 x 16.2 cm.)
Signed lower left: Gustave Moreau
Inscribed and dated lower right:
Rome 1860 Académie de France

Collection:
Musée Gustave Moreau, Paris; Drawings
No. 718

Literature:
For Moreau's work of this type
Anonymous, 1914 , p. 33
Pool, 1963, p. 254

22.
Studies from the Nude and an Académie,
1858
8¼ x 10⅝ in. (21.0 x 27.0 cm.)
Inscribed lower left: Académie Villa
Medicis
Signed, inscribed, and dated lower right:
Gustave Moreau Rome 1858

Collection:
Musée Gustave Moreau; Drawings
No. 719

Literature:
For Moreau's work of this type
Pool, 1963, p. 254

23.
Italian Coast, 1859
Pencil, charcoal, and watercolor on
gray-green paper
6¼ x 8⅝ in. (16.0 x 22.0 cm.)
Inscribed and signed lower left: Naples
Monte Saint Angelo Gustave Moreau
Dated lower right: Juillet 1859

Collection:
Musée Gustave Moreau, Paris; No. 377

Literature:
For general comments on Italian
landscape studies
Laran, 1913, pp. 21-22
Boisse, 1917, p. 420
Lejeaux, 1947, p. 21
Pool, 1963, p. 254
Paladilhe, 1971, pp. 15-16

24.
Roman Landscape, 1858
Pastel on paper
6⁵⁄₁₆ x 9¹⁄₁₆ in. (16.0 x 23.0 cm.)
Signed, inscribed, and dated lower left:
Gustave Moreau Rome 1858

Collection:
Musée Gustave Moreau, Paris; No. 459

Literature:
See cat. no. 23

25.
Autumnal Landscape
Charcoal and watercolor on paper
5⅞ x 9¹⁄₁₆ in. (15.0 x 23.0 cm.)
Signed lower left: Gustave Moreau

Collection:
Musée Gustave Moreau, Paris; No. 328

Literature:
Boisse, 1917, p. 422

26.
Landscape, Etampes, ca. 1885-1886
Charcoal and watercolor on paper
6⁵⁄₁₆ x 4⁵⁄₁₆ in. (16.0 x 11.0 cm.)
Inscribed lower left: Etampes
Initialed lower right: GM

Collection:
Musée Gustave Moreau, Paris; No. 465

Literature:
Boisse, 1917, p. 421

27.
Italian Peasant, Seen from the Back,
ca. 1857-1859
Watercolor on white paper
7½ x 3⅛ in. (19.0 x 8.0 cm.)

Collection:
Musée Gustave Moreau, Paris; No. 479

28.
Oedipus and the Sphinx, 1864
Oil on canvas
81¼ x 41¼ in. (206.4 x 104.7 cm.)
Signed and dated lower left:
Gustave Moreau 64

Collections:
Prince Jérôme Bonaparte (1864)
William H. Herriman, Rome
The Metropolitan Museum of Art (1921)

Exhibitions:
Salon of 1864, No. 1388
Paris, 1961, No. 10
New York, 1961, No. 175

Literature:
Notebook III 21
E. About, *Salon de 1864,* 1864, pp. 137ff
F. Aubert, *Le Pays,* 1864
L. Auvray, *Salon de 1864,* 1864,
pp. 54-57
A. Cantaloube, *Nouvelle Revue de Paris,*
June 15, 1864, pp. 602-607
H. de Callias, *L'Artiste,* 1864, p. 219
M. du Camp, *Revue des Deux Mondes,*
1864, pp. 28-36, 705-712
J. Castagnary, *Salon de 1864,* reprinted
in *Salons (1857-1870),* 1892, I,
pp. 198-202
J. Clarétie, *L'Artiste,* 1864, p. 4
C. Clément, *Journal des Débats,*

May 12, 1864
Drion, *Journal du Soir,* June 8, 1864
Dubosq de Pesquidoux, *L'Union,*
June, 1864
H. Fouquier, *Le Peuple,* May 11, 1864
T. Gautier, *Le Moniteur Universel,*
May 27, 1864
T. Gautier fils, *Le Monde Illustré,*
June, 1864
L. Lagrange, *Gazette des Beaux-Arts,*
XVI, June 1, 1864, pp. 506-508
(illus. opp. p. 506)
O. Merson, *L'Opinion Nationale,*
June 13, 1864
A. Nettement, *La Semaine des Familles,*
1864, pp. 587-588
P. C. Parent, *Le Courrier Artistique,*
May 15, 1864
A. Paul, *Le Siècle,* June 8, 1864
J. Rousseau, *L'Univers Illustré,*
May 28, 1864
P. de Saint-Victor and J. Rousseau,
L'Artiste, 1864, p. 24
P. de Saint-Victor, *La Presse,* May 7, 1864
De Sault, *Le Temps,* May 12, 1864
M. de Thémines, *La Patrie,* June 24, 1864
T. Thoré (W. Bürger), *Salon de 1864,*
reprinted in *Salons de W. Bürger, 1861 à
1868* (1870), II, pp. 14-19, 22
P. Mantz, *Gazette des Beaux-Arts,* XXIII,
1867, p. 330
Chesneau, 1868, pp. 181-190
T. Gautier, *L'Illustration,* LIII, May-June
1869, reprinted in *Tableau à la plume,*
n.d., pp. 279ff
Savarus, 1879
Phillips, 1885, p. 230
Leprieur, I, pp. 169-171, 348, 354,
357, 444, 449f
Larroumet, 1896, pp. 270-271
Thévenin, 1897, p. 14
White, 1897 (illus. p. 5)
Breton, 1899, pp. 178f
Flat, 1899, p. 17
Geffroy, 1900, pp. 3-6
Renan, 1900, pp. 27, 45, 50-52, 181
(illus. opp. p. 40)
O. Redon, in a letter (Jan. 29, 1900),
published in *Lettres d'Odilon Redon,*
1923, p. 38
Schuré, 1904, pp. 369-370
Larroumet, 1904, p. 242
1906, Paris, p. 30
Loisel, 1912, pp. 15, 28
Laran, 1913, pp. 25-28
Desvallières, 1913, pl. 8
Anonymous, 1914, p. 36f
Boisse, 1917, p. 424
C. Léger, *Courbet selon les caricatures
et les images,* Paris, 1920, p. 54
G. Coquiot, *Des Gloires Déboulonnées,*
Paris, 1924, p. 107-109
Rouault, 1926, *Le Correspondent,* p. 141
Praz, 1933, pp. 295-296
Tabarant, 1943, p. 391
C. Chassé, *Le Mouvement Symboliste
dans l'Art du XIXe Siècle,* Paris, 1947,
p. 34
J. C. Sloane, *French Painting between the
Past and the Present,* Princeton, 1951,
pp. 171f., 174 (note 46), 175 (fig. 68)
B. Polak, *Het Fin-de-siècle in de
Nederlandse Schilderkunst,* Amsterdam,

1955, pp. 38f
von Holten, *Symbolister: Tidskrift för
Konstvetenskap,* Malmo, XXII, 1957,
pp. 36-50 (notes), illus. p. 39
von Holten, 1960, pp. 2-9 (fig. 6)
1961, Paris, pp. 27f, No. 10, pl. 6
1961, New York, pp. 115, 179
(illus. p. 113)
von Holten, *Neusser Jahrbuch,* 1964,
pp. 11-33
1964-1965, Tokyo (fig. 5)
Paris, 1965, p. 240
von Holten , 1965, pp. 22-30, 197
(illus. p. 23)
Crespelle, 1966, p. 164 (illus. No. 267)
Margaretta M. Salinger and Charles
Sterling, *French Paintings. A Catalogue
of the Collection of The Metropolitan
Museum of Art, XIX-XX Centuries,*
New York, 1967, vol . III, pp. 1-5
(illus. p. 3)
Carlo Sala, *Max Ernst et la démarche
Onirique,* Paris, 1970, p. 69
Paladilhe, 1971 , pp. 23, 25-26, 75-77,
80, 97 (illus. No. 51)
Dorra, 1973, pp. 130-140 (illus. p. 130)
Frongia, 1973 (fig. 1)
Mizue, 1973 (illus. in color p. 14)

29.
First Idea for Oedipus and the Sphinx,
1861
Pencil, pen , and ink on paper
11⅛ x 5⅝ in. (29.0 x 14.0 cm.)
Inscribed, signed, and dated below:
Premiere idée Gustave Moreau/
GM OEDIPE ET LE SPHINX 1861

Collection:
Musée Gustave Moreau, Paris; Moreau
Museum No. 517

Exhibitions:
Paris, 1961, No. 73
Tokyo, 1964-1965, No. 55

Literature:
Geffroy, 1900, p. 6, illus.
Rouault, *L'Art et Les Artistes,* 1926,
(illus. p. 240)
von Holten, 1960, p. 5
Paris, 1961, pp. 14, 44
Biehler, 1964, cover
von Holten, *Neusser Jahrbuch,* 1964,
p. 41
von Holten, 1965 (illus. p. 26)
Paladilhe, 1971 (illus. No. 7)

30.
*Study for Oedipus and Copy after Ingres'
Oedipus in De Cavalleriis, "Antiquarum
Statuarum Urbis Romae,"* ca. 1860
Pencil on paper
Drawing on left: 1⅝ x 1⅛ in.
(4.0 x 2.7 cm.)
Drawing on right (after Ingres'
Oedipus): 1½ x 1 1/16 in. (3.8 x 2.7 cm.)

Collection:
Musée Gustave Moreau, Paris; Inventory
No. 14629

Literature:
von Holten, 1957, illus. p. 42
von Holten, 1960, figs. 7, 8
von Holten, 1965, p. 26 (repr.)

31.
Oedipus and the Sphinx, ca. 1860
Watercolor on paper
12 9/16 x 8⅝ in. (32.0 x 22.0 cm.)

Collection:
Musée Gustave Moreau, Paris; No. 569

32.
Study for Oedipus
Pencil on paper
10¾ x 9 in. (27.8 x 22.8 cm.)
Inscribed upper right: de la/jointure
du poignet à l'os du/coude
Inscribed left: ne pas se rapporter a
l'ensemble qui n'est past juste
Inscribed center right: os du coude/
mesurant la longueur/ de l'attache de la
hanch/a l'attache du pectoral

Collection:
Musée Gustave Moreau, Paris; Drawings
No. 2840

33.
Study for the Sphinx's Wing in Oedipus
Pencil on paper
11 13/16 x 7⅝ in. (29.9 x 19.4 cm.)

Collection:
Musée Gustave Moreau, Paris; Drawings
No. 2489

34.
Jason and Medea, ca. 1865
Pencil, pen and ink on paper
7 11/16 x 4⅛ in. (19.5 x 10.4 cm.)

Collection:
Musée Gustave Moreau, Paris; Drawings
No. 1754

Literature:
For Moreau's drawings for *Jason and
Medea*
Bengesco, 1913, p. 108

For the large finished oil
C. Blanc, *L'Avenir National,*
June 13, 1865
A. de Bullement, *Les Beaux Arts,*
May 15, 1865
Cham, *Le Salon de 1865 photographié
par Cham,* Paris, 1865 (caricature)
E. Chesneau, *Le Constitutionnel,*
May 9, 1865
C. Clément, *Journal des Débats,*
May 10, 1865
T. Gautier, *Le Moniteur Universel,*
July 9, 1865
M. de Montifaud, *L'Artiste,* May 15, 1865
G. de Mouy, *Revue Française,*
June 1, 1865
Revue des Deux Mondes, June 1, 1865,

pp. 662-663
De Sault, *Le Temps,* May 24, 1865
Thilda, *La Vie Parisienne,* May 6, 1865 and May 13 (caricature)
J. Walter, *L'Entracte,* May 17, 1865
Renan, 1886, p. 40
Leprieur, 1889, pp. 19, 32, 39-40
White, 1897, pp. 4-5
Bénédite, 1899, p. 23
Renan, 1899, vol. 1, pp. 191, 299, 304-306 (illus. p. 18)
Muther, 1901 (illus. p. 299)
Larroumet, 1904, p. 242
Schuré, 1904, pp. 363-364
Desvallières, 1913, No. 37
Laran, 1913, pp. 29-30 (illus. No. VII)
Dreyfus, 1914, p. 170
Anonymous, 1914, pp. 38-39, (color repr.)
Coquiot, 1924, pp. 109-110
Lejeaux, 1947 (illus. p. 15)
Charles Sterling and Hélène Adhemar, *Peintures, Ecole Française, XIXe Siècle, Musée National du Louvre,* Paris, 1961, III, No. 1421, pl. 543
von Holten, 1965, pp. 31-32, 197 (repr. p. 32)
Paladilhe, 1971, pp. 77, 113
1972, London, p. 80, No. 138
Frongia, 1973 (fig. 2b)
Mizue, 1973 (illus. p. 17)

35.
Jason, ca. 1865
Pencil on paper
7½ x 4 5/16 in. (19.0 x 11.0 cm.)
Inscribed lower left: Jason
Signed lower right: Gustave Moreau

Collection:
Musée Gustave Moreau, Paris; Drawings No. 1755

36.
Study for Jason, ca. 1865
Red and white chalk on gray paper
16¼ x 8⅞ in. (41.3 x 22.5 cm.)

Collection:
Musée Gustave Moreau, Paris; Drawings No. 1973

37.
Drapery Study
Pencil and white chalk on gray-brown paper
6 5/16 x 10⅞ in. (16.0 x 27.7 cm.)
Signed and inscribed lower right:
Gustave Moreau — Léda

Collection:
Musée Gustave Moreau, Paris; Drawings No. 1974

38.
Orpheus, ca. 1866
Oil on canvas
39½ x 25½ in. (100.5 x 64.8 cm.)
Initialed: G.M.

Collections:
M. Panckoucke (1906)
Benouville
Germain Seligman
Washington University, St. Louis (1965)

Exhibitions:
1906, Paris, No. 100
1956, Washington, D.C., No. 19
1957, Bordeaux, *Bosch, Goya et la Fantastique,* No. 325
1960, Cambridge, Massachusetts, Busch-Reisinger, *Gustave Moreau — Monticelli,* No. 2
1960, Pittsburgh, Carnegie Institute, *Art Nouveau* (no catalog)

Literature:
For the Salon painting
Notebook II 65
E. About, *Le Petit Journal,* May 18, 1866
A. Cantaloube, *Le Journal Littéraire,* May 21, 1866
E. Chesneau, *Le Constitutionnel,* May 8, 1866
C. Clément, *Le Journal des Débats,* May 15, 1866
L. de Cormenin, *Journal du Loire,* May 20, 1866
M. Du Camp, *Revue des Deux Mondes,* June 1, 1866, pp. 707-709
A. J. Du Pays, *L'Illustration,* May 12, 1866
T. Gautier, *Le Moniteur Universel,* May 15, 1866
M. De Montifaud, "Salon de 1866, I: Peinture et Dessin," *L'Artiste,* 1866
De Sault, *Le Temps,* May 31, 1866
Un Flaneur, *Revue de Paris,* May 15, 1866
M. de Villemer, *Le Figaro,* May 13, 1866
J. Walter, *Gazette des Etrangers,* May 17, 1866
L'Artiste, Jan. 1, 1867, p. 66 (illus. opp. p. 66)
C. Blanc, *Le Temps,* Aug. 27, 1867
E. Chesneau, *Le Constitutionnel,* Sept. 10, 1867
Chesneau, 1868, pp. 202-203
Radiguet, 1868, pp. 80-81
Charles Blanc, *Les artistes de mon temps,* Paris, 1876, p. 468
Leprieur, 1889, pp. 618-619, 25-26
Th. de Wyzewa and X. Perreau, *Les grands peintres de la France,* Paris, 1891, p. 34 (illus.)
Larroumet, 1896, p. 273
Roger-Marx, 1897, p. 62
Thévenin, 1897, pp. 15-17
White, 1897, p. 6
J. d'Udine, "Les Gustave Moreau du Musée du Luxembourg," *La Plume,* February 15, 1899, pp. 196-199
A. Meunier, "Géorgiques," *La Plume,* May 1, 1899, p. 297 (illus.)
Meurville, 1899, p. 65 (illus. p. 66)
J. Rais, "La peinture française pendant le cours du siècle," *Encylopédie du Siècle. L'Exposition de Paris, 1900,* Paris, I, 1900, p. 162 (illus. opp. p. 132)
Renan, 1900, pp. 56-58 (illus.)
Muther, 1901 (illus. p. 297)
Larroumet, 1904, p. 233
Schuré, 1904, pp. 350-351
Hugo Daffner, *Salome Ihre Gestalt in Geschichte und Kunst,* Munich, 1912, pp. 289-290 (illus. p. 282)
Loisel, 1912, pp. 32-33
Bengesco, 1913, pp. 109-110
Desvallières, 1913, No. 27
Laran, 1913, pp. 35-36
Anonymous, 1914, pp. 43-44 (color illus.)
Dreyfus, 1914, p. 172
Coquiot, 1924, pp. 110-111
Orliac, 1926, p. 15
Rouault, 1927, p. 42
Lejeaux, 1947 (illus. p. 19)
Beurdeley, 1955, illus. p. 40
Sandstrom, 1955, pp. 45-48
A. Breton, *L'art magique,* Paris, 1957, p. 214 (illus.)
von Holten, 1960, pp. 11-13 (illus. in color pl. 11)
Biehler, 1964 (illus. opp. p. 91)
1964-1965, Tokyo (fig. 1)
Paris, 1965, p. 237
Schiff, 1965 (illus. p. 352, p. 359)
von Holten, 1965, pp. 34, 197 (illus. p. 35, pp. 71-72)
J. Milner, *Symbolists and Decadents,* London and New York, 1971, p. 38 (illus. p. 39)
Paladilhe, 1971, pp. 34, 99, 124 (illus. No. 10)
M. Proust, *Essais et articles (Notes sur le monde mysterieux de Gustave Moreau)* included in *Contre Sainte Beuve,* Paris, ed. Pléiade, 1971, p. 671
1972, London, pp. 15, 80-81 (illus. in color pl. 1, illus. No. 140)
Frongia, 1973, pp. 397, 400 (fig. 22)
Mizue, 1973 (illus. in color, p. 15)

39.
Orpheus, ca. 1866
Pencil on paper
10 1/16 x 6⅝ in. (25.5 x 17.0 cm.)
Signed lower left: Gustave Moreau
Inscribed lower right: Orpheus

Collection:
Musée Gustave Moreau, Paris; Drawing No. 2894

40.
The Poet and the Saint, 1868
Watercolor on paper
Monogrammed and signed lower left:
Gustave Moreau
Inscribed lower center:
LE POETE ET LA SAINTE
11⅜ x 6½ in. (27.5 x 10.0 cm.)

Collections:
Alexandre Dumas Fils, Paris (Sale, Paris,
Hôtel Drouot, March 2-3, 1896,
No. 107)
Leopold Goldschmidt, Paris
Drs. Fritz and Peter Nathan, Zurich
Norton Simon Inc. Museum of Art,
Los Angeles (Sale, New York, Sotheby
Parke-Bernet, Oct. 22, 1968, No. 5,
plate 2)
Harriet Griffin Gallery, New York
Piccadilly Gallery, London

Exhibition:
Salon of 1869, no. 2990

Literature:
E. Hache, *Les Merveilles de l'Art et de
l'Industrie (Salon 1869),* Paris, 1869,
p. 315
Leprieur, 1889, p. 17
Paul Flat, "Gustave Moreau," *Revue de
l'Art Ancien et Moderne,* III,
March 10, 1898, p. 232 (repr. p. 233)
Schuré, 1904, pp. 351-352
Laran, 1913, pp. 41-42 (illus. pl. XIII)
Anonymous, 1914, p. 49
Coquiot, 1924, pp. 112
Petibon, 1931, p. 207
Paladilhe, 1971, pp. 34, 99

41.
Prometheus, 1868
Oil on canvas
80 x 48⅝ in. (205.0 x 122.0 cm.)
Signed and dated lower left:
Gustave Moreau: 1868
Inscribed lower right: Prometheus

Collection:
Musée Gustave Moreau, Paris; No. 196

Exhibition:
Salon of 1869, no. 1746

Literature:
Notebook 11, 19, 29, 73
E. Bellangé, *Le Progrès de Rouen,*
May 20, 1869
Bertall, *Journal Amusant,* May 29, 1869
(caricature)
C. Blanc, *Le Temps,* May 19, 1869
A. Bonnin, "Salon de 1869, III Les
Peintres d'Histoire," *La France,*
May 23, 1869
J. Bosier, *Fantaisie Parisienne,*
May 31, 1869
E. Chesneau, "Salon de 1869, Peinture I
(Suite) MM. Chenavard et Gustave
Moreau," *Le Constitutionnel,*
June 1, 1869
C. Clément, *Journal des Débats,*
May 14, 1869
H. Fouquier, "Le Salon de 1869," *Revue
internationale de l'art et de la curiosité,*
June 15, 1869
T. Gautier, *L'Illustration,* May 15, 1869
J. Paul, *La Gazette de France,*
May 13, 1869
A. de Pontmartin, *L'Univers Illustré,*
May 18, 1869
Leprieur, 1889, pp. 37-38
Castagnary, *Salons,* 1892, Vol. I, p. 368
Thévenin, 1897, p. 17

Flat, 1899, p. 16 (unnumbered plate)
Geffroy, 1900, pl. II
Renan, 1900, pp. 86-88
Musée Gustave Moreau, 1904, pp. 10-11,
46 (illus. opp. p. 62)
Schuré, 1904, pp. 376-377
Loisel, 1912, p. 34
Desvallières, 1913, No. 11
Laran, 1913, pp. 45-46
Anonymous, 1914, pp. 52-54
(color illus.)
Dreyfus, 1914 (illus. p. 175)
Coquiot, 1924, pp. 112-113
Lejeaux, 1947 (illus. p. 18)
von Holten, 1960, pp. 13-14 (fig. 16)
Biehler, 1964, p. 80 (illus. opp. p. 103)
von Holten, 1965, pp. 37-39, 197
(illus. p. 38)
Paladilhe, 1971, pp. 34, 77

42.
Salome Dancing Before Herod, 1876
Oil on canvas
56⅝ x 41 1/16 in. (143.8 x 104.2 cm.)

Collections:
Louis Mante, Marseilles (Sale, Paris,
Galerie Charpentier, Nov. 28, 1956,
no. 10)
Robert Lebel, Paris
Julius Weitzner, London (1958)
Huntington Hartford, New York (Sale,
New York, Sotheby Parke-Bernet
Galleries, March 10, 1971, no. 29)
Armand Hammer, Los Angeles

Exhibitions:
Paris, *Salon of 1876,* no. 1506
Paris, *Exposition Universelle
Internationale,* 1878, no. 657
Paris, Galerie Georges Petit, *Gustave
Moreau Exposition au Profit des Oeuvres
du Travail et des Pauvres Honteux,*
1906, no. 76
New York, 1961-1962, No. 177
Oklahoma City, San Diego, Los Angeles,
The Armand Hammer Collection,
1971-1972, No. 29

Literature:
Notebook III, 49, 63; IV 55, 67
Edmond About, *Le 19e Siècle,*
May 28, 1876
Ariste, *L'Indépendance Belge,*
May 18, 1876
Emile Bergerat, "Salon de 1876,"
Journal Officiel, May 12, 1876
Emile Bergerat, *Journal du Loiret,*
Orléans, May 19, 1876
Emile Blavet, *Le Gaulois,* June 21, 1876
Ernest Boysse, *La Patrie,* May 25, 1876
Castagnary, *Le Siècle,* May 20, 1876
Victor Cherbuliez, "Le Salon de 1876,"
Revue des Deux Mondes, June 1, 1876,
pp. 521-522

Ernest Chesneau, *La Gazette,* May 8, 1876
Jules Claretie, *La Presse,* May 16, 1876
Charles Clément, "Exposition de 1876,"
Journal des Débats, May 13, 1876
Alfred Darcel, *Journal de Rouen,*
May 6, 1876
Charles Darcours, *Journal Illustré,*
May 21, 1876
Edouard Drumont, *La Gazette,*
May 7, 1876
George Dufour, "Le Grand Art et le
Petit Art du Salon de 1876," *L'Artiste,*
Amiens, pp. 24-25
Judith Gautier, "Le Salon II," *Le Rappel,*
May 6, 1876
La Gazette de France, June 15, 1876
Louis Gonse, *La Nouvelliste de Rouen,*
May 8, 1876
Gabriel Guillemot, "Salon de 1876,"
Le Soleil, May 10, 1876
George Lafenestre, *Le Moniteur
Universel,* May 12, 1876
Paul Mantz, *Le Temps,* May 21, 1876
Le Monde Illustré, May 27, 1876
P. H., *L'Avenir de la Sarthe,* Le Mans,
June 17, 1876
Laurent Pichat, *La Phare de la Loire,*
Nantes, May 22, 1876
Alex Pothey, *La Corsaire,* May 20, 1876
S***, "Salon de 1876," *L'Electeur du
Finistère,* Brest, June 28, 1876
P. de Saint-Victor, "Salon de 1876,"
La Liberté, May 19, 1876
Pierre de Savarus, "Le Salon de 1876,
a Vol d'Oiseau,* Paris, 1876, pp. 43-44
Victor de Swarte, *Lettres Sur le Salon
de 1876,* St. Omer, 1876, p. 79
Marius Vachon, *La France,* May 24, 1876
Von Heym, *La Défense,* May 30, 1876
Albert Wolff, "Quatrième Promenade
au Salon," *Le Figaro,* May 12, 1876
Charles Yriarte, "Le Salon de 1876,"
Gazette des Beaux Arts, 13, June 1, 1876,
pp. 705-708 (p. 698 illus.)
Zig Zags, *Salon de 1876, Gustave
Moreau,* June 25, 1876, No. 9, p. 2
E. Bergerat, *Les Chefs-d'Oeuvre d'Art à
l'Exposition Universelle 1878,* Paris,
1878, p. 156 (illus. pl. 20)
Charles L. Duval, *Les Beaux-Arts à
l'Exposition de 1878 Impression et Notes
d'Artistes,* Meaux, 1878, p. 127
*Exposition Universelle de Paris, 1878,
Le Livre d'Or des Exposants,* Section I
(Beaux-Arts), Paris, 1878, p. 10
Hippolyte Gautier and Adrien Desprez,
Les Curiosites de L'Exposition de 1878,
Paris, 1878, p. 87
Paul Mantz, "Paris Exposition
Universelle, La Peinture Française,"
Gazette des Beaux Arts, I, Dec. 1, 1878,
p. 47
Mario Proth, *Les Artistes Français à
l'Exposition Universelle de 1878,* Paris,
1878, p. 56
Paul Mantz, "L'Art Moderne a
l'Exposition de 1878," *Gazette des
Beaux-Arts,* Paris, 1879, pp. 31, 33
Savarus, 1879, pp. 89-91
Dubosc de Pesquidoux, *L'Art dans les
Deux Mondes, Peinture et Sculpture
(1878),* Paris, 1881, Vol. I, p. 82
Huysmans, J. K. *A Rebours,* Paris,
1884 (1959, Penguin), pp. 63-67

Leprieur, 1889, Mar. pp. 175, 177, 180, May pp. 339, 350, 351, June pp. 444, 449, 450, 452
Castagnary, 1892, II, pp. 227-228
Larroumet, 1896, pp. 277-278
Thévenin, 1897, pp. 9, 12-13
White, 1897, p. 11
Bénédite, 1899, pp. 265-290, p. 273 (illus.)
Renan, 1900, pp. 62-64, 68-71 (illus.)
Gustave Geffroy, *La Vie Artistique*, 6th series, chap. XVI, Paris, 1900, pp. 143-147
Frantz, 1900, pp. 99-104
Gustave Larroumet, *Notice Historique sur la vie et les oeuvres de M. Gustave Moreau*, Institut de France, Paris, 1901, pp. 21, 22, 29, 30 (illus. p. 36)
F., H., 1902, p. 268 (illus.)
1906, Paris, p. 19, 38
Symons, 1906, pp. 73-77
Hugo Daffner, *Salome Ihre Gestalt in Geschichte und Kunst*, Munich, 1912, pp. 289-290
Loisel, 1912, p. 52
Laran, 1913, pl. XXVIII, pp. 71 (illus. opp. p. 72)
Desvallières, 1913, No. 9 (illus.)
Anonymous, 1914, pp. 69-70
Coquiot, 1924, pp. 115-116
Rouault, *L'Artet les Artistes,* 1926, p. 223 (illus.)
Duthuit, 1954 (illus., p. 31)
Praz, 1956 (original copyright 1933), pp. 291-293
von Holten, 1957, illus., p. 48
von Holten, 1960, pp. 18-20, pl. III, p. 27 (illus. in color)
von Holten, 1961, pp. 44-51, 72
1961-1962, New York, p. 118-119
John Simon, "The Torments of Imagination," *Arts,* Feb. 1962, pp. 20-27 (illus.)
1964-1965, Tokyo (fig. 3)
von Holten, 1965, pp. 48-53, 197 (illus., p. 49)
Max Gérard, *Dali,* New York, 1968, no. 169 (detail illus. in color)
Kaplan, 1970, pp. 393-394
Helen Osterman Borowitz, "Visions of Salome," *Criticism,* Detroit, XIV, I, Winter 1972, pp. 14-15 (illus.)
Frongia, *Commentari,* 1972, pp. 146-147 (fig. 4)
Los Angeles, London, Dublin, 1972, *The Armand Hammer Collection* (illus. in color no. 29)
Frongia, 1973, pp. 397, 399-400 (fig. 3)
Mizue, 1973 (illus., p. 39)
Meyers, 1974, pp. 39-41, fig. 3, pl. VI

43.
Study for Salome Dancing Before Herod, ca. 1875
Pencil on tracing paper
13⅝ x 3¹⁵/₁₆ in. (34.9 x 9.9 cm.)

Collection:
Musée Gustave Moreau, Paris; Drawings No. 2274

44.
Study for Herod in Salome Dancing Before Herod, ca. 1875
Pencil, pen and ink on tracing paper
13¹¹/₁₆ x 10⅜ in. (34.9 x 26.3 cm.)
Inscribed upper right:
— un oiseau — un serpent apprivoisé/ ou un éventail-/ — Il tient un oiseau-/ — chercher par un moyen/quelconque à enlever à/cette figure toute apparence/ de majesté et de dignité/bien qu'elle doive être/impassible/Momie orientale extenuée & sommeillante/aspect sacerdotal/hieratique idole/ — Le Tétraque chef/politique et religieux
Inscribed lower right:
Dans mes dessins Indiens/Album
Inscribed lower left:
(indecipherable) de sousbassement (sic) /pour l'escabeau sous les pieds d'Hérode/voir Villemin 1ᵉʳ vol. page 59 — idem. sousbassement (sic) page 66
Signed and inscribed lower left:
Gustave Moreau — Salomé dansant

Collection:
Musée Gustave Moreau, Paris; Drawing No. 2275

45.
Study for Salome in Salome Dancing Before Herod, ca. 1872-1875
Pencil, pen and ink on tracing paper
18 x 8⅝ in. (45.8 x 21.8 cm.)
Signed lower left: Gustave Moreau
Inscribed lower right: Salomé

Collection:
Musée Gustave Moreau, Paris; Drawings No. 2276

46.
Study for the Executioner in Salome Dancing Before Herod, ca. 1872-1875
Pencil on tracing paper
17 x 6¹¹/₁₆ in. (43.2 x 15.8 cm.)
Inscribed lower left: Gustave Moreau

Collection:
Musée Gustave Moreau, Paris; Drawings No. 2277

47.
Study for Salome Dancing Before Herod, ca. 1872-1875
Oil on panel
12⅝ x 9⅞ in. (32.0 x 25.0 cm.)

Collection:
Musée Gustave Moreau, Paris; No. 751

48.
Study for Salome Dancing Before Herod, ca. 1872-1875
Pencil on paper
9 x 10⁹/₁₆ in. (22.8 x 26.8 cm.)
Signed lower left: Gustave Moreau
Inscribed below middle: Salome
Inscribed lower right: d'après le mannequin

Collection:
Musée Gustave Moreau, Paris; Drawings No. 2307

49.
Salome
Pencil and charcoal on paper
23⁴/₁₆ x 13⁹/₁₆ in. (59.0 x 34.5 cm.)
Initialed lower left: GM

Collection:
Musée Gustave Moreau, Paris; Moreau Museum Inventory No. 13966
Exhibition:
Paris, 1961, No. 89
New York, 1961, No. 196

Literature:
Flat, 1899, unnumbered plate
von Holten, 1960, p. 20 (illus. fig. 20)
von Holten, 1961 (p. 46 illus.)
1961, Paris (fig. 45)
von Holten, 1965 (repr. p. 55)
Paladilhe, 1971, p. 84 (illus. No. 65)
Lake, 1972 (illus. p. 8)

50.
Hercules and the Hydra of Lerna, 1876
Oil on canvas
69 x 60½ in. (75.3 x 53.5 cm.)
Signed lower right: Gustave Moreau

Collections:
Louis Mante, Marseille (Sale, Paris, Galerie Charpentier, Nov. 28, 1956)
Richard L. Feigen, Chicago
Jacques Seligmann & Co., New York
Art Institute of Chicago, 1964

Exhibitions:
Salon of 1876, No. 1505
Exposition Universelle, Paris, 1878, Groupe I, Classe I, No. 656
1906 Paris, No. 75
Lawrence, Kansas, University of Kansas, *Profiles and Perspectives in 19th Century French Art,* Jan. 14-Feb. 26, 1958, No. 18
1961, New York, No. 178
1969, Minneapolis, Minnesota, The Minneapolis Institute of Arts, *The Past Rediscovered: French Painting 1800-1900,* July 1-Sept. 7, No. 62

Literature:
Edmond About, *Le 19e Siècle,*
May 28, 1876
Ariste, *L'Independance Belge,*
May 18, 1876
Arthur Baignières, *L'Echo Universel,*
May 15, 1876
Emile Bergerat, "Salon de 1876," *Journal Officiel,* May 12, 1876
Emile Bergerat *Journel du Loiret,*
Orléans, May 19, 1876
Emile Blavet, *Le Galois,* June 2, 1876
Ernest Boysse, *Le Patrie,* May 25, 1876
Castagnary, *Le Siècle,* May 20, 1876
Victor Cherbuliez, "Le Salon de 1876,,"
Revue des Deux Mondes, June 1, 1876,
pp. 520-521
Ernest Chesneau, *La Gazette,* May 8, 1876
Jules Claretie, *La Presse,* May 16, 1876
Charles Clément, "Exposition 1876,"
Journal des Débats, May 13, 1876
Alfred Darcel, *Journal de Rouen,*
May 6, 1876
Charles Darcours, *Journal Illustré,*
May 21, 1876
Edouard Drumont, *La Gazette,*
May 7, 1876
George Dufour, "Le Grand Art et Le Petit Art au Salon de 1876," *L'Artiste,*
Amiens, 1876, p. 24
Judith Gautier, "Le Salon II," *Le Rappel,*
May 6, 1876
La Gazette de France, June 15, 1876
Louis Gonse, *Le Nouvelliste de Rouen,*
May 8, 1876
Gabriel Guillemot, "Salon de 1876,"
Le Soleil, May 10, 1876
George Lafenestre *Le Moniteur Universel,*
May 12, 1876
Paul Mantz, *Le Temps,* May 21, 1876
Albert Merat, *Le Petit Salon,* Paris, 1876,
p. 18
Le Monde Illustré, May 27, 1876
P. H., *L'Avenir de la Sarthe,* Mans,
June 17, 1876
Louis Pichat, *Le Phane de la Loire,*
Nantes, May 22, 1876
Alex Pothey, *Le Corsaire,* May 20, 1876
Mario Proth, *Voyage au Pays des Peintres.
Salon 1876,* Paris, 1876, p. 123
S***, "Salon de 1876," *L'Electeur du Finistère,* Brest, June 28, 1876
Paul de Saint-Victor, "Salon de 1876,"
La Liberté, May 19, 1876
Armand Silvestre, *L'Opinion,*
May 8, 1876
Stradella, *Le Français,* May 15, 1876
Victor de Swarte, *Lettres sur le Salon de 1876,* Paris, 1876, p. 79
Marius Vachon, *La France,* May 24, 1876
Von Heym, *La Défense,* May 30, 1876
Albert Wolff, "Quatrième Promenade au Salon," *Le Figuro,* May 12, 1876
Charles Yriarte, "Le Salon de 1876,"
Gazette des Beaux Arts 13, June 1, 1876,
pp. 705-706
Emile Bergérat, *Les Chefs d'Oeuvre d'Art a l'Exposition Universelle de 1878,*
pp. 156-157
Charles L. Duval, *Les Beaux-Arts à l'Exposition Universelle de 1878,* Paris,
1878, p. 127
Paul Mantz, *L'Art Moderne a l'Exposition Universelle de 1878,* Paris, 1879, p. 31
Mario Proth, *Les Artistes Français a l'Exposition Universelle de 1878,* p. 56
Savarus, 1879, pp. 89, 92-93
Dubosc de Pesquidoux, *L'Art dans les Deux Mondes, Peinture et Sculpture (1878),* Paris, 1881, Vol. I, p. 82
Leprieur, 1889, pp. 36-37
Castagnary, 1892, II, p. 228
White, 1897 (illus., p. 11)
Bénédite, 1899, p. 27
Flak, 1899, p. 23
Renan, 1900, pp. 88-91 (illus., p. 89)
Gustave Larroument, *Notice Historique sur la vie et les oeuvres de M. Gustave Moreau,* Institut de France, Paris, 1901,
pp. 15, 59
F., H., 1902 (illus. p. 273)
Schuré, 1904, pp. 326, 359-360
1906, Paris, p. 19
Loisel, 1912, p. 34
Devallières 1913, No. 12 (illus.)
Laran, 1913, pp. 67-68 (illus. pl. XXVI)
Dreyfus, 1914, p. 174
Anonymous, 1914, p. 68
Coquiot, 1924, p. 115
Blanche, 1931, p. 96
von Holten, 1960, p. 27 (illus. fig. 29)
1961, New York, pp. 116, 118 (color illus., p. 117)
Paris, 1965, pp. 240-241
von Holten, 1965 (illus., p. 67)
Paladilhe, 1971, p. 123
Frongia, *Storia dell'arte,* 1972, pp. 86-87,
Ill. 4

51.
Apollo and Python
Oil on panel
9 x 6 in. (23.0 x 15.3 cm.)

Collections:
Marie Raffalovich, Paris
Faerber and Maison, Ltd., London
National Gallery of Canada,
Ottowa (1969)

Literature:
Mizue, 1973 (illus., p. 38)

52.
Study for Hercules and the Hydra of Lerna, ca. 1869-1875
Charcoal on buff paper
7¹³⁄₁₆ x 6 in. (19.8 x 15.2 cm.)

Collection:
Musée Gustave Moreau, Paris;
Drawings No. 2097

53.
Study for Hercules and the Hydra of Lerna, ca. 1869-1875
Pencil on paper
3¾ x 4¾ in. (9.5 x 12.0 cm.)

Collection:
Musée Gustave Moreau, Paris;
Drawings No. 2098

54.
Study for Hercules and the Hydra of Lerna, ca. 1869-1875
Pencil on white paper
3⁹⁄₁₆ x 3¹⁵⁄₁₆ in. (9.0 x 10.0 cm.)

Collection:
Musée Gustave Moreau, Paris;
Drawings No. 2099

55.
Calvary, 1867
Oil on canvas
9⁷⁄₁₆ x 12⁹⁄₁₆ in. (24.0 x 32.0 cm.)
Monogrammed, signed and dated lower left: V&/Gustave Moreau, 1867

Collection:
Charles Hayem, Paris
Louvre (May 16, 1898)

Exhibitions:
1906, Paris, No. 86
1962, Mexico, *Cien anos de pintura en Francia de 1850 a nuestros daes*
1963, *Bordeaux, Delacroix, ses maîtres, ses élèves,* May 17-Sept. 30, No. 369

Literature:
Leprieur, 1889, p. 47
Renan, 1900, pp. 118, 131
Mauclair, 1905, *The Art Journal*
(illus., p. 256)
1906, Paris, p. 20
Loisel, 1912, pp. 57-58
Laran, 1913, p. 62
Blanche, 1931, p. 133
Charles Sterling and Hélène Adhémar, *Peintures Ecole Française XIXe Siècle Musée National du Louvre,* Paris, 1961,
No. 1422
Crespelle, 1966 (illus. 270)

56.
St. Sebastian, ca. 1878
Pencil, charcoal, and sanguine on paper
24³⁄₁₆ x 14¹⁄₁₆ in. (61.5 x 35.8 cm.)

Collection:
Musée Gustave Moreau, Paris;
Drawings No. 827

Exhibition:
1974, Okayama, Hiroshima, Tokyo

Literature:
For finished oil in Fogg Museum
Bénédite, 1899, p. 165
Musée Gustave Moreau, 1904, illus. bet.,
pp. 122-123
Anonymous, 1914, p. 68
For the theme in general
Loisel, 1912, p. 77
Paladilhe, 1971, p. 65

57.
Jacob and the Angel, ca. 1878
Watercolor on paper
7³⁄₁₆ x 4 in. (18.5 x 10.0 cm.)
Signed lower left: Gustave Moreau

Collection:
Musée Gustave Moreau, Paris; Moreau
Museum Inventory No. 13988

Literature:
For the theme in general, see Schuré,
1904, pp. 368-369
Notebook II 45
Desvallières, 1913, pp. 81-82, No. 34
(illus.)
von Holten, 1960 (fig. 65)
von Holten, 1965, p. 118
For the original oil in the Fogg Museum
Savarus, 1879, pp. 87-89
Leprieur, 1889, p. 37
Renan, 1900, pp. 72, 74
Schuré, 1904, pp. 368-369
Larroumet, 1904, p. 237
1906, Paris, p. 30
Loisel, 1912, pp. 35-36 (illus. p. 11)
Bengesco, 1913, pp. 110-111
Laran, 913, pp. 81-82
Coquiot, 1924, p. 116
Biehler, 1964, p. 63
Paladilhe, 1971, p. 134

58.
David, ca. 1878
Oil on canvas
38$\frac{15}{16}$ x 21$\frac{1}{4}$ in. (98.0 x 54.0 cm.)

Collection:
Musée Gustave Moreau, Paris; No. 199

Literature:
For the finished oil
Notebook II 55, 56; III 77, 79, 91; IV 46
Dubosc de Pesquidoux, *L'Art dans les
Deux Mondes, Peinture et Sculpture
(1878),* Paris, 1881, vol. 1, p. 84
Laran, 1913, pp. 79-80, No. XXXIII
(illus.)
Paul Mantz "L'Art Moderne à
L'Exposition de 1878," *Gazette des
Beaux-Arts,* 1879, pp. 31-33
Savarus, 1879, pp. 94-95
Phillips 1885, pp. 228-233 (illus.)
Leprieur, 1889, p. 40
Lorrain, 1895, p. 67
Renan, 1900, pp. 71-73 (illus.)
Frantz, 1900, pp. 97-104 (illus. p. 98)
Gustave Larroumet *Notices historiques
sur la vie et les oeuvres de M. Gustave
Moreau,* Institut de France, Paris, 1901,
p. 36
Dimier, 1902, p. 276
Catalogue, Musée Gustave Moreau, 1904,
p. 47
Camille Mauclair, "The Gustave Moreau
Museum in Paris," 1905, *The Art
Journal,* London, p. 255 (illus.)
Loisel, 1912, p. 41
Desvallières, 1913, No. 22 (illus.)
Laran, 1913, pp. 79-80, pl. XXXII
Anonymous, 1914, p. 74
Coquiot, 1924, p. 116
von Holten, 1960, p. 29, pl. 37

von Holten, 1965, p. 71
Paladilhe, 1971, p. 123
Los Angeles, 1972, No. 28
Mizue, 1973, illus. p. 39

59.
Saint Cecilia, ca. 1877
Pen and ink, and oil on panel
19$\frac{11}{16}$ x 13$\frac{3}{4}$ in. (50.0 x 35.0 cm.)

Collection:
Musée Gustave Moreau, Paris; No. 754

Exhibition:
1964, Baden-Baden, No. 94

Literature:
Notebook II 95
Bénédite, 1899, p. 21
Renan, 1900, p. 119
Loisel, 1912, p. 76
Paladilhe, 1971, pp. 65-67

60.
Study of Animal Skull, 1881
Pencil on paper
7$\frac{13}{16}$ x 5$\frac{1}{2}$ in. (19.8 x 14.0 cm.)
Inscribed and dated lower left: lion de
barberie/Jardin des Plantes/Galeries
d'anatomie comparée/10 septembre 1881

Collection:
Musée Gustave Moreau, Paris;
Drawings No. 1274

61.
Study of Animal Skull, ca. 1879-1886
Pencil on white paper
7 x 10$\frac{5}{8}$ in. (17.8 x 27.0 cm.)
Signed lower left: Gustave Moreau

Collection:
Musée Gustave Moreau, Paris;
Drawings No. 1275

62.
Study of Animal Skull, ca. 1879-1886
Red and lead pencil, charcoal on
cream paper
7$\frac{13}{16}$ x 13$\frac{3}{4}$ in. (19.8 x 35.0 cm.)
Signed lower left: Gustave Moreau

Collection:
Musée Gustave Moreau, Paris;
Drawings No. 1276

63.
Phoebus and Boreas, 1879
Watercolor
11$\frac{3}{8}$ x 8$\frac{1}{4}$ in. (29.0 x 21.0 cm.)
Signed lower right: Gustave Moreau

Collection:
Musée Gustave Moreau, Paris; No. 492

Exhibitions:
1949-50, Paris, No. 115
1962, Marseille, No. 8
1964-65, Tokyo, No. 100 (illus. pl.
LXXXIX)
1969, Turin, Galleria Civica d'Arte
Moderna *Il sacro il profano nell'arte dei
simbolisti,* No. 77 (illus.)

1969, Toronto, Art Gallery of Toronto,
*The Sacred and Profane in Symbolist
Art,* No. 62
1972, London, No. 171

Literature:
Catalogue, Musée Gustave Moreau,
1904, No. 492
1906, Paris, p. 22
Laran, 1913, p. 100
1972, London, p. 90
Mizue, 1973 (illus. in color p. 51)

64.
*Study for a Figure in Hercules and the
Daughters of Thestius,* 1883
Pencil on white paper
13$\frac{3}{8}$ x 7$\frac{1}{2}$ in. (34.0 x 19.0 cm.)
Inscribed and dated lower left:
Rosa Dejessi/Thestius/2 août 83
Signed lower right: Gustave Moreau

Collection:
Musée Gustave Moreau, Paris;
Drawings No. 2233

65.
*The Dragon with Many Heads and the
Dragon with Many Tails,* ca. 1879-1881
Pencil on buff paper
11 x 8$\frac{7}{16}$ in. (28.0 x 21.5 cm.)

Collection:
Musée Gustave Moreau, Paris;
Drawings No. 2607

Literature:
For finished fable
Laran, 1913, p. 100
Jullian, 1969 (illus. 2)

66.
The Lion and the Gnat, ca. 1879-1881
Charcoal and black wash on blue paper
11$\frac{1}{4}$ x 8$\frac{7}{16}$ in. (28.5 x 21.3 cm.)

Collection:
Musée Gustave Moreau, Paris;
Drawing No. 2605

Literature:
For the finished fable
1906, Paris; p. 24
von Holten, *L'Oeil,* 1964 (illus.)

67.
The Mogul's Dream, ca. 1879-1881
Pencil, pen and ink on tracing paper
10$\frac{3}{8}$ x 8 in. (26.4 x 20.2 cm.)

Collection:
Musée Gustave Moreau, Paris;
Drawing No. 2606

Literature:
For the finished fable
Leprieur, 1889, p. 50
Larroumet, 1896, p. 281
Renan, 1900, p. 112
Larroumet, 1904, p. 241
1906, Paris, p. 21
von Holten, 1960, p. 38 (illus. fig. 53)
von Holten, L'Oeil, 1964 (illus.)
von Holten, 1965, p. 102 (illus.)
Paladilhe, 1971, p. 134

68.
The Monkey and the Leopard,
ca. 1883-1886
Pencil on yellow paper
11¹³⁄₁₆ x 8¼ in. (30.0 x 20.9 cm.)

Collection:
Musée Gustave Moreau, Paris;
Drawings No. 2608

Literature:
1906, Paris, p. 25
von Holten, L'Oeil, 1964 (illus.)

69.
The Peacock Complaining to Juno,
ca. 1881-1882
Watercolor
Signed lower left: Gustave Moreau
11⅜ x 7½ in. (29.0 x 19.0 cm.)

Collection:
Anthony Roux, Marseille
Madame Goldschmidt, Paris
Musée Gustave Moreau, Paris; Moreau
Museum No. 566 bis

Exhibitions:
1886, Paris, Galerie Goupil, *Exposition
des aquarelles de Gustave Moreau*
1906, Paris, No. 143
1961, Paris, No. 108
1964, Neuss, No. 33 (illus. 11)
1964-1965, Tokyo, No. 62 (illus. in color
pl. XXXVII)

Literature:
Renan, 1900, p. 112 (illus. p. 111)
1906, Paris, p. 23
Laran, 1913, p. 99
1961, Paris, p. 52
Paris, 1965, p. 236
von Holten, 1965, p. 108
Paladilhe, 1971, p. 134

70.
The Wolf and the Lamb, ca. 1883-1886
Pencil and watercolor on paper
11 x 7½ in. (28.0 x 19.0 cm.)

Collection:
Musée Gustave Moreau, Paris; Moreau
Museum No. 300

Literature:
For the finished fable
Larroumet, 1896, p. 281
1906, Paris, p. 25
Laran, 1913, p. 98

71.
The Frogs Asked for a King,
ca. 1883-1886
Pencil and watercolor on paper
12³⁄₁₆ x 7⅞ in. (31.0 x 20.0 cm.)

Collection:
Musée Gustave Moreau, Paris; No. 448

Literature:
For the finished fable
1906, Paris, p. 25
von Holten, L'Oeil, 1964 (illus.)

72.
Hercules and the Doe
Watercolor
8¾ x 6 in. (22.0 x 14.0 cm.)
Signed lower right: Gustave Moreau

Collection:
Musée Gustave Moreau, Paris; No. 320

Exhibitions:
1961-1962, New York, No. 206
1964-1965, Tokyo, No. 79 (illus. pl.
LXXXIV)

73.
Dante and Virgil
Watercolor
6⁵⁄₁₆ x 9¹³⁄₁₆ in. (16.0 x 25.0 cm.)

Collection:
Musée Gustave Moreau, Paris; No. 470

Exhibition:
Baden-Baden, 1964, No. 38

74.
The Prodigal Son
Watercolor
4¾ x 11⁷⁄₁₆ in. (12.0 x 29.0 cm.)
Signed lower left: Gustave Moreau
Inscribed lower right: L'Enfant Prodigue

Collection:
Musée Gustave Moreau, Paris; No. 417

Exhibitions:
Louvre, 1961, No. 97
Baden-Baden, 1964, No. 33

Literature:
For a general discussion of the theme
Loisel, 1912, p. 51

75.
Centaurs Carrying a Dead Poet
Watercolor
14⁵⁄₁₆ x 9⁷⁄₁₆ in. (36.3 x 24.0 cm.)
Signed lower right: Gustave Moreau

Collection:
Musée Gustave Moreau, Paris; No. 484

76.
The Siren and the Poet, 1896-1899
Tapestry
137½ x 94½ in. (349.0 x 250.0 cm.)

Collections:
Commissioned by the State (1894)
Sent to the Musée du Luxembourg
(1901)
Transferred to the Musée National d'Art
Moderne (1939)
Transferred to the Mobilier National
(1969)

Exhibitions:
1900, *Universal Exhibition,* Paris,
Group XII, Class 70
1961, Paris, No. 145
1971, Sèvres, Musée National de
Céramique, L'Art de la poterie de Rodin
à Dufy, p. 13
1972, London and Liverpool, No. 190

Literature:
Bénédite, "Deux Idealistes," 1899,
Frontispiece
Renan, Nov. 1899, p. 432
F. Calmettes, "L'Exposition Universelle.
Les tissus d'Art," *La Revue de l'Art
Ancien et Moderne,* Oct. 1900,
pp. 243-244 (illus. 24)
J. Guiffrey, "La Manufacture des
Gobelins à l'Exposition de 1900,"
Encyclopédie du siècle, 1900, pp. 268,
270, 276 (illus. No. 35 following
p. 276)
J. Guiffrey, "La Manufactures des
Gobelins à l'Exposition de 1900," *Art
et Decoration,* I, 1900, p. 154 (illus.
p. 149)
L. Bénédite, *Exposition Universelle
Internationale de 1900 a Paris, Rapport
du Jury International. Introduction
générale. Deuxième partie. Beaux-Arts,*
Paris, 1904 (illus. p. 697)
von Holten, 1960, p. 29
1961 — Paris, p. 63
von Holten, 1965, p. 75
Paladilhe, 1971, p. 60
London and Liverpool, p. 95
Frongia, 1973, fig. 9

77.
The Triumph of Alexander the Great,
ca. 1890
Oil, watercolor, tempera on canvas
61 x 61 in. (155.0 x 155.0 cm.)
Signed lower right: Gustave Moreau
Inscribed lower right: Alexandre

Collection:
Musée Gustave Moreau, Paris; No. 70

Exhibitions:
1961, Paris, No. 43
1967, Hotel Meurice, *Manifeste en
Hommage à Meissonnier,* Nov. 1-30
1972, London and Liverpool, No. 149

Literature:
Notebook II 63
Flat, 1899, p. 23-24
Renan, 1900, pp. 124, 125
Larroumet, 1901, p. 38
Catalogue, Musée Gustave Moreau, 1904,
p. 27 (illus. opp. p. 10)
1906, Paris, p. 7
Huneker, 1910, p. 354
Loisel, 1912, pp. 18-19
Desvallières, 1913, No. 38
Laran, 1913, p. 111
Anonymous, 1914, p. 79
Boisse, 1917, p. 423
Lorrain, 1929, pp. 268, 271, 272
von Holten, 1960, p. 27, fig. 35
1961, Louvre, p. 38
Grojnowski, 1963, p. 237
Berger, 1964 (illus. no. 68)
Biehler, 1964 (illus. opp. p. 66)
Schiff, 1965, pp. 356-357, 359
von Holten, 1965, p. 68 (illus. p. 70)
Jullian, 1969 (illus. p. 161)
Paladilhe, 1971, pp. 83, 151, 153, 161
Lake, 1972 (illus. p. 8)
1972, London, p. 83 (illus. no. 149)
Frongia, 1973 (fig. 30)
Mizue, 1973 (illus. p. 30)

78.
Detail for the Triumph of Alexander,
ca. 1890
Pencil, brush, and ink on tracing paper
14¹⁄₁₆ x 17¾ in. (35.8 x 45.0 cm.)
Reversed inscription center below: à
rechercher l'elephant de la Bastille dessin
d'Alavoi *(sic.)*

Collection:
Musée Gustave Moreau, Paris
Moreau's inscription refers to the drawing
by Jean Antoine Alavoine of a fountain
in the form of an elephant for the Place
de la Bastille in Paris. (See Charles
Le Blanc, *Manuel de l'Amateur
D'Estampes,* Paris, 1854-1888, I, p. 7.)

79.
Orestes and the Erynnies, 1891
Oil on canvas
70 x 48½ in. (180.0 x 120.0 cm.)
Signed lower right: Gustave Moreau
(not in exhibition)

Collections:
Anthony Roux, Marseilles (Sale, Galerie
Georges Petit, Paris, May 19, 1914,
No. 23, p. 19 illus.)
André Germain, Paris (Sale, Sotheby,
London, Nov. 7, 1962)
James F. Covington Jr., California
Mr. and Mrs. Stephen Higgins, Paris
Giovanni Agnelli, Turin

Exhibitions:
Paris, 1961, No. 44
Turin, (Galleria Civica d'Arte Moderna)
1967-1968, *Le Muse Inquietanti,
Maestri del Surrealismo,* No. 16 (illus.)

Literature:
Notebook II, 61
Renan, 1900, pp. 81-85 (illus. p. 131)

Gustave Larroumet, *Notice historique
sur la vie et les oeuvres de M. Gustave
Moreau* (Institut de France), Paris, 1901,
p. 38
Mauclair, *The Art Journal,* 1905, p. 254
1906, Paris, p. 20
Loisel, 1912, p. 19
Desvallières, 1913, pl. No. 42
Dreyfus, 1914, p. 176
von Holten, 1960, p. 28 (fig. 39)
1961, Paris, p. 38
Schiff, 1965, p. 360
Paris, 1965, pp. 239-240
von Holten, 1965 (illus. p. 69)
Crespelle, 1966, p. 164
Paladilhe, 1971, p. 118
Frongia, *Storia dell'arte,* 1972, pp. 85-86,
(fig. 3)
Frongia, 1973, p. 397 (fig. 24)

80.
Oil Sketch
Oil on panel
14⁹⁄₁₆ x 18⁵⁄₁₆ in. (37.0 x 46.5 cm.)

Collection:
Musée Gustave Moreau, Paris; No. 1135

Exhibitions:
1961, New York, No. 192
1964-1965, Tokyo, No. 31 (illus. in
color pl. XII)

Literature:
For a general discussion of the oil
sketches
Cremona, 1955
Ashton, 1961
Jenkins, 1961
Ragon, 1961
Grojnowski, 1963, p. 235
Frongia, *Commentari,* 1972

81.
Oil Sketch
Oil on panel
9⁹⁄₁₆ x 8⅝ in. (24.3 x 21.9 cm.)

Collection:
Musée Gustave Moreau, Paris; No. 1153
Literature:
See cat. no. 82

82.
Oil Sketch
Oil on wood
12⁹⁄₁₆ x 15¾ in. (32.0 x 40.0 cm.)

Collection:
Musée Gustave Moreau, Paris; No. 1140

Exhibition:
1964-1965, Tokyo, No. 26 (illus.
pl. XCI)

83.
The Good Samaritan
Oil on canvas
28⁵⁄₁₆ x 39⅜ in. (82.0 x 100.0 cm.)

Collection:
Musée Gustave Moreau, Paris; No. 78

84.
The Ideal Flower, The Catholic Church,
ca. 1890-1898
Charcoal and watercolor
13¾ x 9⁷⁄₁₆ in. (35.0 x 24.0 cm.)
Inscribed and signed on bottom: La Fleur
Ideale Ecclesia Catholica — Gustave
Moreau

Collection:
Musée Gustave Moreau, Paris;
Drawings No. 974

85.
St. John of the Apocalypse, 1896
Pencil and watercolor on white paper
4¾ x 3⅝ in. (12.0 x 9.3 cm.)
Dated, inscribed, and signed below:
1896 — Saint Jean De L'Apocalipse —
Gustave Moreau

Collection:
Musée Gustave Moreau, Paris;
Drawings No. 843

86.
Argonautes, ca. 1897
Watercolor
13¼ x 8⅝ in. (33.7 x 22.0 cm.)
Initialed lower right: GM

Collection:
Musée Gustave Moreau, Paris;
Drawings No. 844

Exhibition:
Louvre, 1961, No. 118

Literature:
Notebook II 51; IV 36
Paris, 1961, p. 54
For the large oil of the same subject
Geffroy, 1900 (illus. pl. IV)
Les Maîtres Artistes, 1901, illus. p. 19
Catalogue, Musée Gustave Moreau, 1904,
p. 6 (illus. bet. pp. 2 and 3 opp. p. 18)
Desvallières, 1913, No. 54
Romanet, 1926, p. 313
von Holten, 1960 (illus. fig. 34)
von Holten, 1965, p. 68-69 (repr. p. 71)
Paladilhe, 1971, pp. 60, 64, 132
Frongia, *Storia dell'arte,* 1972, p. 91
(illus. 9)
Frongia, 1973 (fig. 12)
Mizue, 1973 (illus. p. 33)

87.
Jupiter and Semele, 1889
Oil on canvas
31½ x 21⅝ in. (80.0 x 55.0 cm.)
Dated and signed lower left:
1889/Gustave Moreau

Collection:
Musée Gustave Moreau, Paris; Moreau
Museum No. 94

Exhibition:
1961, Paris, No. 42
1964-1965, Tokyo, No. 44

Literature:
For this work
von Holten, 1965 (illus. p. 88)
Frongia, *Commentari,* 1972, p. 145
(fig. 8)
Frongia, 1973 (fig. 34)
Mizue, 1973 (illus. p. 29)
For the finished oil
Notebook II 41; IV 16, 55
Larroumet, 1896, p. 288
Flat, 1899, pp. 23-24
Renan, 1900, 93, 126
Schuré, 1904, pp. 372-373
Catalogue, Musée Gustave Moreau, 1904,
p. 2 (illus. opp. p. 2)
Loisel, 1912, pp. 15, 34-35
Bengesco, 1913, pp. 99-101
Desvallières, 1913, No. 40
Laran, 1913, p. 109
Lajeaux, 1947, pp. 19-20
Duthuit, 1954 (illus. p. 29)
Breton, 1957, p. 214
von Holten, 1960, pp. 34-36 (illus. in
color pl. V)
Anonymous, 1961, illus. in color p. 68
Grojnowski, 1963, p. 227
Restany, 1964 (illus. pp. 82, 95)
1964-1965, Tokyo (illus. pl. XXIX)
Paris, 1965, pp. 231-234 (illus.)
Schiff, 1965, pp. 360, 376-377 (illus.
pp. 377-380)
von Holten, 1965, pp. 71, 83-92, 97
(illus. p. 84)
Kaplan, 1970, pp. 393-414
Paladilhe, 1971, pp. 45, 60, 64, 111, 123,
128, 130
Frongia, *Storia dell'arte* 1972, pp. 88-90
(illus. 7, 8)
Frongia, 1973, pp. 398, 402-3 (fig. 10)
Mizue, 1973 (illus. in color p. 23)

88.
*Study for Bacchus and Semele for Jupiter
and Semele,* ca. 1890
Pencil on paper
16¾ x 11¹¹⁄₁₆ in. (42.5 x 29.7 cm.)
Signed lower left: Gustave Moreau
Inscribed lower center: De la part de
Delaunay 21 ans/Antoinette Grillard —
7 rue des/Martyrs — très fine — très-/
jolie d'ensemble — jolie tête./pouvra bien
servir pour la figure de Sémélé
Inscribed lower right: SEMELE
The inscription refers to the common
practice among Moreau and his artist
friends of sharing models that were
especially pleasing. Here he refers
specifically to his friend, Elie Delaunay
(1828-1891).

Appendix I:
The Fables of La Fontaine

English titles are taken from Marianne Moore's translation of *The Fables of La Fontaine* (New York, 1954).

Judith Gautier's review of the 1881 exhibition listed the following twenty-five Fables (*Le Rappel,* May 19, 1881):

1.
Frontispiece
2.
Phoebus and Boreas
3.
The Lion in Love
4.
The Lion and the Gnat
5.
The Peasant from the Danube
6.
The Rats in Council
7.
The Miser and the Monkey
8.
Discord
9.
Death and the Woodman
10.
The Ape and the Dolphin
11.
The Mouse Metamorphosed into a Maid
12.
The Farmer and the Adder

13.
The Oyster and the Litigants
14.
The Two Adventurers and the Talisman
15.
The Mogul's Dream
16.
The Two Friends
17.
The Dragon with Many Heads and the Dragon with Many Tails
18.
The Grasshopper and the Ant
19.
The Matron of Ephesus (This was one of La Fontaine's stories rather than a fable.)
20.
For Those Impossible to Please
21.
Democritus and the People of Abdera
22.
The Two Mules
23.
Jupiter and the Thunderbolts
24.
The Town Rat and the Country Rat
25.
The Torrent and the River

The remaining thirty-nine works of the series were done between May 1881 and their date of exhibition in 1886. Seven of them, Nos. 26 through 32 were finished during the eight months after the exhibition, that is by January 1882. And five more, Nos. 33 through 37, were probably done at the same time since they appeared on a list that Moreau had drawn up that contained the previous seven watercolors. Of this group, only Nos. 31, and 34 through 36 are known by titles.

26.
The Stag and the Horse Who Would Be Revenged
27.
The Peacock's Complaint to Juno
28.
The Vultures and the Pigeons
29.
The Elephant and Jupiter's Monkey
30.
The Lion and the Rat
31.
Jupiter and the Wayfarer
32.
The Rat and the Elephant
33.
The Cobbler and the Financier
34.
Bertrand and Ratto (The Monkey and the Cat)
35.
The Lion (The Leopard)
36.
The Lion Grown Old
37.
The Thieves and the Ass

Moreau finished Nos. 38 and 39 shortly after December 15, 1882.

38.
The Animals Sick of the Plague
39.
The Two Doves

The remaining twenty-four fables were all finished between 1883 and 1886, but their chronology is not sure. According to Moreau's lists the next group was probably Nos. 40 through 48.

40.
The Wolf and the Lamb
41.
The Man Who Ran after Fortune and the Man Who Waited for Her at Home
42.
The Fox and the Stork
43.
The Miller, His Son, and the Ass
44.
The Cock and the Pearl
45.
The Monkey and the Leopard
46.
The Shepherd and the Sea
47.
The Oak and the Reed
48.
The Old Man and the Ass
49.
The Dairymaid and Her Milk-Pot
50.
The Bear and the Two Schemers
51.
The Bear and the Garden-Lover
52.
The Companions of Ulysses
53.
The Tortoise and the Two Ducks
54.
The Frog Who Would be an Ox
55.
The Frogs Asked for a King
56.
The Coach and the Fly
57.
An Animal in the Moon
58.
The Fox and the Crow
59.
The Fox and the Grapes
60.
Love and Folly
61.
The Head and Tail of the Serpent
62.
The Cat Changed to a Woman
63.
The Donkey and the Relics
64.
Fortune and the Child

Notebook II

II, 38
La Grèce seule . . . rêve à son génie et
poursuit son idéal . . . appuyé sur
l'instrument éternel de la pensée humaine
— la lyre.

II, 41-44
Au centre d'architecture aérienne
colossale, sans bases ni faîtes couverts
de végétations animées et frémissantes,
flore sacrée se découpant sur les sombres
azurs des voûtes étoilées des déserts
(solitudes) du ciel.

Le Dieu tant de fois invoqué, se manifeste
dans sa splendeur encore voilée.

Sémélé pénétrée des effleuves divins,
régénérée, purifiée par ce sacre, meurt
foudroyée, et avec elle le génie de l'amour
terrestre, le génie aux pieds de bouc.

Alors sous cette incantation et cet
exorcisme sacré, tout se transforme,
s'épure, s'idéalise, l'Immortalité
commence, le divin se répand en tout, et
tous les êtres ébauchés, encore informes,
aspirent à (adorent — vont à) la vraie
lumière — Satyres, faunes, dryades,
hamadryades, hôtes des eaux et des bois,
tous sont atteints, éperdus de joie,
d'enthousiasme et d'amour, se dégageant
de leur limon terrestre, ils aspirent
(vont) aux sommets montant, montant
toujours, prenant quelques uns déjà la
forme des génies supérieurs, des génies
religieux (sacrés) aux ailes éployées aux
attitudes d'officiants sont en adoration
devant le Dieu.

Au pied de ce trône La Mort et La
Douleur forment cette base tragique de
la Vie (de l'Humanité) humaine et non
loin d'elles, sous l'égide de l'Aigle de
Jupiter, le Grand Pan, symbole de la terre,
courbe son front attristé dans un regard
d'esclavage et d'exil, tandis qu'à ses
pieds s'entasse la sombre phalange des
monstres de l'Erèbe et de la Nuit, des
êtres non formés de l'Ombre et du
Mystère, les indéchiffrables énigmes des
ténèbres.

La Lune silencieuse et fatale, l'Hécate aux
regards égarés (obliques), les griffons,
les lemures, les hydres de sang, monstres
aux formes hybrides, divinités fatales
(funestes) de la nuit, sommeillant au
fond du gouffre et dans les abîmes de
l'ombre.

Et les deux Grands Sphynx qui sont le
passé, et l'avenir gardiens de ce
formidable troupeau de l'Erèbe et des
solitudes (avenues) célestes, se
contemplent l'un l'autre dans leur
immobilité (rigide au sourire figé)
souriante et hiératique.

La mort et l'apothéose et l'immortalité.

C'est une ascension vers les sphères
supérieures, une montée des êtres épurés,
purifiés vers le divin — La mort terrestre
et l'apothéose dans l'immortalité. Le
grand mystère s'accomplit — toute la
Nature est imprégnée (pénétrée)
d'idéal et du divin — tout se transforme.

C'est un hymne à la divinité.

Des atomes de parcelles de Christianisme
apparaissent dans cette composition —
Cette mort des sens, cette ruine de l'être
matériel pour entrer dans la vie
immortelle. Cette allégresse des êtres à
l'apparition de la lumière divine, au
contact de l'idéal divin, tout cela sont son
Christianisme. Le Paganisme est flétri
dans son essence par un renversement,
une déviation de son symbolisme. Signé
GM 10 8bre 97

II, 45
Jacob et l'ange — La lutte, il cherche à
deviner à travers l'immense nuit l'énigme
mystérieuse et sacrée de la vie et sa
force impuissante ne pourra rien saisir.

Mais l'Ange envoyé de Dieu qui a pitié de
l'homme, souriant à ses efforts stériles,
incline son coeur par l'Amour, le soumet
et bientôt l'inonde des splendeurs
(clartés) eternelles.

II, 55-56
C'est lui qui va rendre au poète et sa
lyre et son saint enthousiasme et qui va le
consoler dans son immense tristesse en
lui apportant la manne divine et
immortelle (en lui donnant l'amour).
L'amour du Dieu de bonté tout puissant
et des choses eternelles.

II, 63-64
Alexandre — Le jeune roi conquérant
domine tout ce peuple captif, vaincu et
rampant à ses pieds, dompté de crainte et
d'admiration — La petite vallée indienne
où se dresse le trône immense et superbe
contient l'Inde entière, les templex aux
faîtes fantastiques, les Idoles terribles —
les lacs sacrés — les souterrains pleins
de mystères et de terreur et toute cette
civilisation inconnue et troublante . . . le
jeune Grec tend son sceptre vers le roi
vaincu en signe de grace (clemence) et de
protection souveraine.

Et la Grèce et l'esprit et l'âme de la
Grèce triomphent au loin — et l'âme de la
Grèce rayonnante et superbe triomphe
au loin dans les régions inexplorées du
mystère et du rêve. Signé GM 10 8bre 97

II, 73
Or je veux rendre l'homme de sacrifice
et de pensée aux prises, dans la vie, avec
les tortures et les attaques de la brutalité
et de la matière vile, je n'irais pas suivant
la logique du sentiment . . . faire de
l'Aigle, le plus noble et le plus royal des
animaux, le bourreau et le tortionnaire
de cette figure résignée.

II, 75-76
Les Lyres mortes — les poètes, les chantres
païens meurent de cet embrassement,
de cette absorption ardente avec la matière
sous les formes créées par eux . . . mourant
sans cesse pour renaître plus vivace,
absorbant, détruisant tout autour d'elle,
sereine, silencieuse, pleine de mystère,
animée, pénétrée créée vivante par
l'imagination, l'adoration, la lyre du
poète païen.

Mais la grande lyre de l'âme, la grande
voix aux cordes vibrantes de l'idéal
vraiment divin vient éteindre (abolir)
toutes ces voix des sens, ces voix de la
Nature glorifiée; elle se dresse cette lyre
superbe, tenue par l'archange sombre et
terrible armé de la croix de sang qui
va régénérer le monde, cette croix,
sublime symbole du sacrifice, du mépris
des choses éphémères, et témoignage
suprême d'adoration de l'éternel divin
. . . 24 Xbre 97 soir — Noël Signé GM

II, 82
J'ai choisi pour la tête maîtresse de
l'animal le serpent hadji, adoré par les
Egyptiens, ce qui me permet de lui
donner cet aspect immobile et inquiétant
dans la fixité, tandis que les autres reptiles
greffés sur son corps [illegible] ne sont
que les instruments ou membres de sa
colère, se tordent de fureur exprimant la
passion intérieure de la bête.

II, 95
Ste. Cecile — Au crépuscule du soir, la sainte écoute les voix célestes des chérubins, sa rêverie vivante et visible. L'heuhe est mélancolique et l'expression de douce tristesse répandue sur le visage de la jeune fille, est comme une manifestation du pressentiment de ses destinées futures glorieuses et tragiques.

Cette composition est presque un pendant à celle du David

Ce sont des rêveries aux deux pôles de la vie. La rêverie souriante de la jeune fille et la rêvasserie sévère du vieillard . . .

II, 96
L'impression de ce petit ouvrage . . . reside en somme dans le choix des tonalités, dans les valeurs et dans l'arabesque des lignes principales qui donnent à la composition un caractère presque religieux.

Toutes les descriptions n'y feront rien maintenant reste à savoir si la peinture éveille dans l'esprit du spectateur une impression quelconque sans l'aide des descriptions. Là est le point capital.

Notebook III

III, 3-4
Au rebours des juges ordinaires qui prétendent, qu'en fait d'art, (dans une oeuvre manuscrite) toutes les parties doivent être soumises au même style pour satisfaire aux lois de l'harmonie, je dirai qu'il y a deux sortes d'harmonie: l'harmonie du bon sens et celle de l'imagination.

Les grands peintres dans l'emploi de leurs matériaux pour une oeuvre d'art, n'ont jamais suivi la logique de l'esprit ou du jugement, mais seulement celle du sentiment et l'on va voir par un seul exemple à quel point ils étaient dans la vérité supérieure, celle du génie:

Poussin[115] ayant à représenter un peuple très ancien et très primitif, d'une ville superbe et fameuse, selon les poètes, livré aux horreurs de la famine ou de la peste; comment pouvait-il, s'il n'avait recours à ce que j'appellerai l'Allégorie Archéologique? Comment, dis-je pouvait-il exprimer l'idée de richesse, de grandeur, de noblesse dans son architecture? C'est seulement en ayant recours à l'anachronisme — et par un bonheur inouï, dont le génie seul jouit, il trouvait moyen de fondre ensemble, sans effort, et pour la plus grande satisfaction imaginative, les civilisations les plus opposées et les plus extrêmes. Exemple de la peste des Philistins.

III, 4-5
. . . C'est le peintre de la raison et du bon sens par excellence. Eh bien! malgré tout, la puissance imaginative l'emporte toujours chez lui. Si l'on veut bien étudier son oeuvre on verra que, malgré son désir d'être vrai, exact, logique, raisonnable . . . il ne peut jamais résister à ses entraînements féconds et souverains, qui le poussent vers cette vérité relative du sentiment, vers cette logique sublime de l'imagination pure, si distante de la logique du bon sens et de la raison.

III, 7-8
Une chose domine chez moi, l'entraînement et l'ardeur la plus grande vers l'abstraction. L'expression des sentiments humains, des passions de l'homme m'intéresse, sans doute, vivement; mais je suis moins porté à exprimer ces mouvements de l'âme et de l'esprit qu'à rendre pour ainsi dire visibles les éclairs intérieurs qu'on ne sait à quoi rattacher, qui ont quelque chose de divin dans leur apparente insignifiance et qui, traduits par les merveilleux effets de la pure plastique, ouvrent des horizons vraiment magiques, je dirai même sublimes.

III, 19
Jason — le coeur des héros — jeune — (dans sa jeunesse) éclate sonore comme une fanfare de guerre. La gloire n'est pour lui qu'un procès . . .

III, 21
Oedipe et le Sphinx — Le peintre suppose l'homme arrivé à l'heure grave et sereine de la vie, se trouvant en présence de l'énigme éternelle. Elle le presse à l'étreinte sous sa griffe terrible — mais le voyageur, fier et tranquille dans sa force morale, la regarde sans trembler.

C'est la chimère terrestre, vile comme la matière et attractive comme elle — représentée par cette tête charmante de la femme avec ses ailes . . . [illegible] de l'idéal, mais le corps du monstre, du Carnassier qui déchire et anéantit . . .

Mais l'âme forte et ferme défie les ( )* bestiales du monstre. L'homme ( ) et ferme défie les atteintes ennivrantes et brutales de la matière et l'oeil fixé sur l'idéal, il marche confiant vers son but après l'avoir foulé aux pieds.

III, 49
Cette femme qui représente la femme éternelle, oiseau léger, souvent funeste traversant la vie, une fleur à la main, à la recherche de son idéal vague. Souvent terrible et marchant toujours foulant tout aux pieds, même des génies et des saints, & cette danse s'exécute, cette promenade mystérieuse s'accomplit devant la mort qui la regarde incessamment béante et attentive, et devant le bourreau à l'épée qui frappe. C'est l'emblème de cet avenir terrible, réservé aux chercheurs d'idéal sans nom, de sensualité et de curiosité malsaine.

III, 50
C'est parce que j'ai ces hautes idées que j'arrive à donner à mes scènes ce caractère indécis et mystérieux qui étonne et stupéfie tant de gens sans cervelle.

III, 54
. . . ne parler à l'imagination que par l'arabesque de la figure ou du groupe . . .

*I have used ( ) to note the spaces in Moreau's manuscript.

III, 57
Il faut dire, pourtant, que la façon toute sculpturale et toute épique dans laquelle est conçue ce groupe appelle aussitôt l'idée allégorique . . .

III, 63
Cette petite aquarelle d'aujourd'hui m'a montré d'une façon admirable que je ne fais bien que quand je travaille sur des choses faites à la diable.

III, 77
David — c'est encore un sujet sublime: Ce grand roi, ce prophète arrivé aux bornes de la Vie, représentant ces grands vieillards de génie qui ont prié, pleuré, aimé, chanté. Ces grands poètes touchant à l'infini et sur le point d'y entrer. C'est l'heure solennelle, l'heure où toute leur vie leur apparait comme néant, malgré sa grandeur, en la comparant à leur rêve d'immortalité et de divin.

L'Ange personnification vivante de son âme attend le moment de l'inspiration sublime, un moment arrêtée par les mélancoliques pensées et par les découragements de la vie. Il écoute et cette âme qui a conservé sa jeunesse, sa naïveté et sa sensibilité enfantines est bien représentée par ce jeune enfant souriant à demi, à travers ses larmes.

III, 93-94
On revient à cet art primitif, à cet art de la fin du moyen-âge, si différent de celui de la Renaissance, proprement dit, par cette raison seule: c'est que cet art primitif est bien plus près de l'état de notre âme moderne que cet autre art decoratif et sensuel.[116]

Voyez les têtes des primitifs, Giotto, Masaccio, Filippo Lippi, même Botticelli, qui est un peintre sensuel, et vous comprendrez à quel point ces expressions de physionomie, ces caractères de tête sont bien plus faits pour l'âme moderne que les types créés par les Raphaël, les Corrège et les Michel-Ange — Quelle gravité, quelle tristesse, quel mystère dans la Nature et (peut-être à cause de cela) l'idéal n'est plus seulement plastique, rien de l'antiquité, rien du paganisme (sauf les grandes lois du modelé et des plans). La Vie intense, la vie intime de l'Etre avec ses passions, sa manière d'être toute humaine, toute terrestre et, cependant toute idéale toujours et bien souvent divine et le méditatif au-delà de l'expression — C'est très attendrissant — Voyez-vous cet art qui se retrempe et qui se refond à ses sources humaines — Cet idéal prêt à s'évaporer && dans ses prétentions de fluidité idéale et dans ses aspirations supra-terrestres mal définies et absolument vagues, qui reprend pied en interrogeant l'âme triste, l'âme silencieuse dans ses mystères, l'âme — ce trait d'union entre l'homme et Dieu — C'est vraiment très beau, très saint que cette virginité retrouvée.

III, 118

... quand la matière orgueilleuse, quand l'âme basse des avides et des sensuels veut prendre le pas dans cette nouvelle civilisation, sur l'âme et la pensée, je ne me sens que du mépris et de la haine au coeur.

Que ces grands mythes antiques ne soient pas continuellement traduits en historiographies, mais en poèmes éternels, car il faut enfin sortir de cette dironologie puérile qui force l'artiste à traduire les temps limités au lieu de traduire la pensée éternelle — pas la chronologie de l'ésprit. Donner aux mythes toute l'intensité qu'ils peuvent avoir en ne les réservant pas dans des époques et dans des moules et des styles d'époque.

III, 120

Ce sont de pauvres niais prétentieux et tendus, pourris d'orgueil imbécile, ruinés dans leurs moëlles physiques et intellectuelles qui confondent la passion terrestre, l'érotisme, etc., etc., avec la passion artistique, la passion créatrice. Ils n'ont jamais soupçonné ce qu'il faut d'efforts surhumains, de volonté supérieure chez le créateur d'art pour s'élever jusqu'à cette région supérieure où même la plus terrible passion, les violences les plus ardentes se dégagent des basses sensualités pour prendre ce caractère divin et abstrait qui ennoblit et transfigure l'âme. Ce qu'on appelle l'art.

III, 120-124

Et puis il ne faut jamais oublier que je suis français et qu'au nom du bon sens français je n'ai jamais pu rien me permettre dans le sens de la fantaisie, du

rêve idéal, de l'audace à cette poursuite du rare, sur ces chemins flanqués de précipices, plein de fondrières et d'épines sans recevoir de rudes coups de férules. J'ai toujours entendu, tout près de mon oreille, cette voix de la critique saine et juste et qui me faisait douter de tout ce que je tentais et qui m'avertissait que mes imaginations confinaient à la folie ou au gâtisme. C'est donc très difficile pour ne pas dire impossible de pouvoir apprécier ce qu'un producteur aurait pu donner, laissé libre, sinon encouragé dans ses tentatives d'art . . .

Il y a aujourd'hui à ce moment de fausse audace et de fausse ardeur artistique, quand tous les farceurs déshérités cherchaient à attirer par tous les moyens l'attention et le suffrage de la foule et des connaisseurs niais, il y a, dis-je un reproche (une pierre) que l'on jette sans cesse à la tête du véritable artiste et du modeste producteur consciencieux.

. . . En effet, y a-t-il une veille, un jour même ou un lendemain pour une oeuvre immortelle ou durable — . . .

. . . le faux, l'éphémère est toujours ce qui paraît le plus vraiment original aux yeux des imbéciles — . . . les oeuvres saines, intelligibles, nobles et de tradition, bien que parfaitement originales, seront jugées . . . oeuvres vieilles et passées de mode — . . .

Notebook IV

IV, 10-11

Toutes les figures de Michel-Ange semblent être fixées dans un geste de somnambulisme idéal.

C'est en effet, presqu' inconscientes du mouvement qu'elles exécutent dans l'ensemble de la composition, qu'on les voit se mouvoir et agir.

Trouver l'explication de cette répétition presque générale dans toutes ces figures du caractère du sommeil. Donner les raisons de cette rêverie absorbée au point de les faire paraître toutes endormies ou emportées vers d'autres mondes que celui que nous habitons.

Sublimité de cette combinaison plastique. Moyens puissants d'expression dans cette combinaison unique; le sommeil dans l'attitude.

Absorption de l'individu par le rêve.

C'est ce seul sentiment de rêverie profonde qui sauve ces figures de la monotonie, mettant à part, bien entendu, les sublimités du style dans la forme et la science répandue dans ces figures. [117]

Quels actes accomplissent-elles, que pensent-elles, où vont-elles, sous l'empire de quels sentiments sont-elles? L'idée divine, immatérielle, l'idée d'une autre sphère à laquelle elles ont l'air d'appartenir ou d'aspirer, car tout, chez elles, est pour nous mystère.

On ne se repose pas, on n'agit pas, on ne marche pas, on ne médite pas, on ne pleure pas, on ne pense pas de cette façon sur notre planète, dans notre monde. Le geste est toujours explicable dans toute oeuvre plastique dans l'essentiel [illegible] le geste, l'attitude extérieure du corps est toujours en contradiction avec l'expression à rendre de . . . {sic} (admirable ressource plastique) . . .

IV, 17, 19

Cet effort vers le beau pur a pu . . . développer un sens très rare de l'exquis et presque du divin chez certains artistes qui ont fortifié l'étude de ce certain antique par l'étude de la nature et de la vérité absolue.

IV, 20

Croyez-vous en Dieu?
Je ne crois qu'à lui seul.
Je ne crois ni à ce que je touche, ni à ce que je vois.
Je ne crois qu'à ce que je ne vois pas et uniquement à ce que je sens.
Mon cerveau, ma raison me semble éphémère et d'une réalité douteuse; mon sentiment intérieur seul me paraît éternel et incontestablement certain.

IV, 25

On sent, on aime, on sait l'Art, mais on n'en parle pas. Il n'y a pas d'exemple d'un grand homme ayant parlé de son art — de Phidias, de Dante, de Shakespeare, de Mozart, de Raphael, de Vinci, de Poussin & pas un mot — deux lignes de Poussin pour plaire à M. de Chambray, avec ce sous-entendu d'un homme qui sent bien qu'il n'y a rien à dire avec des mots dans une question où les oeuvres seules prouvent, démontrent, déterminent tout.

IV, 31
Jamais on n'a pu voir génération, une
jeunesse aux instincts, aux goûts, aux
allures, aux moeurs plus positifs et jamais
on n'a vu de pareils enthousiasmes
pour l'invisible, des besoins aussi exclusifs
de rêve, de mystère, de mysticisme, de
symbolisme et de non défini. Quel
snobisme! Quelle pose, quel horrible
cabotinisme, charlatanisme et crétinisme!
et ils croient nous en imposer et vous
faire admirer leur goût exquis, rare &
unique.

IV, 36
Les Argonautes — Ivresse ensommeillée —
sur le navire Argo toute la jeunesse
héroique de la Grèce sous la conduite de
Jason rentre au port hellénique. Le navire
porte tous les espoirs, tous les rêves,
toutes les illusions, toutes les chimères
de la jeunesse.

IV, 61
Mon plus grand effort, mon unique souci,
ma préoccupation constante est de
diriger du mieux que je puis, cet attelage
si difficile à conduire d'un pas égal:
mon imagination sans frein et mon esprit
critique jusqu'à la manie.

IV, 113-114
La Nature donne la clef et les lois de
cette science — avant tout il faut beaucoup
la consulter; pour se renseigner et se
munir pour cette partie de l'art.

Manuscript note in the Moreau Museum
not inscribed in the notebooks: ainsi
dans ma Salomé je voudrais rendre une
figure de sybille et d'enchanteresse
religieuse avec un caractère. J'ai alors
conçu le costume qui est comme une
châsse.

Footnotes

115
In his manuscript note Moreau had
originally added "Raphael etc." but he
went back and marked it out.

116
He is undoubtedly referring to his soul,
rather than that of his age.

117
From here on the passage appears only
in Moreau's manuscript note.

Bibliography

Archives: Paris
Archives Nationales. Series F²¹ 99, 164, 241, 2142
Ecole des Beaux-Arts.
"Peinture et Sculpture,
Jugement-Extraits,"
February 1847 to August 1874.
Personal Dossier
Collège Rollin
"Distribution des Prix,"
1831-1840

Moreau's Autograph Writings

Notebooks I, II, III, IV (transcriptions
from his original notes by Henri Rupp
and Jean Paladilhe), Moreau Museum.
Letters in the Bibliothèque Nationale,
Salle des Manuscrits: Papiers
Bracquemond 3, Papiers Dumas IV, Vie
de Robert de Montesquiou, Autographes
Félix et Paul Nadar XX, Papiers
Alexandre Dumas Fils, Correspondance
III, Lettres à Mme. Dumas Fils.
Notice sur M. G. Boulanger,
Paris, 1890.
(This pamphlet records the speech
Moreau gave at the meeting of November
22, 1890 of the Académie des Beaux-Arts,
Institut de France.)
Wright, Barbara and Moisy, Pierre.
*Gustave Moreau et Eugène Fromentin
Documents Inédits.*
La Rochelle, 1972.

Major Studies

Anonymous.
Gustave Moreau.
Paris, 1914.
(Les Peintres Illustres No. 55)
Bou, Gilbert.
Gustave Moreau à Decazeville.
Rodez, 1964.
Cadars, Pierre.
Les Débuts de Gustave Moreau,
1848-1864. June, 1965
(Mémoire, Université de Toulouse).
Desvallières, Georges.
L'Oeuvre de Gustave Moreau.
Paris, 1913.
Flat, Paul.
Le Musée Gustave Moreau.
Paris, 1899.
Laran, Jean and Deshairs, Léon (intro.).
Gustave Moreau,
Paris, 1913. (L'Art de Notre Temps)
Leprieur, Paul.
"Gustave Moreau et Son Oeuvre."
L'Artiste.
Paris, Année 59, I (1889):
161-180, 338-359, 443-455.
Off-print renumbered.
Paladilhe, Jean.
Gustave Moreau.
Paris, 1971.
Pierre, José.
*Gustave Moreau au regard changeant
des générations* (in Paladilhe).
Renan, Ary.
Gustave Moreau, 1826-1898.
Paris, 1900.
Schiff, Gert.
"Die Seltsame Welt des Malers,
Gustave Moreau." *Du Atlantis,*
Zurich, May 1965.
Thévenin, Léon.
L'Esthétique de Gustave Moreau.
Paris, 1897.
Von Holten, Ragnar.
L'Art Fantastique de Gustave Moreau.
Paris, 1960.
Gustave Moreau, Symbolist.
Stockholm, 1965.

General, on Moreau

Anonymous.
"The Splendrous Art of Gustave
Moreau." *Life,*
July 21, 1961.
Anonymous.
"A St. Sebastian by Gustave Moreau,"
Bulletin of City Art Museum of St. Louis,
New Series IV/3 (1968): 1-3.
Ashton, Dore.
"Gustave Moreau." *Odilon Redon,
Gustave Moreau, Rodolphe Bresdin.*
New York, 1961.
Bénédite, Léonce.
*Deux Idéalistes Gustave Moreau
et E. Burne-Jones.*
Paris, 1899.
Nôtre Art nos Maîtres,
Paris, 1922. For Moreau see esp.
pp. 156-181.
Beurdeley, Cécile.
"Gustave Moreau 1826-1898."
Connaissance des Arts 45 (1955): 38-43.

Bierhler, Paul.
"Gustave Moreau ou
l'éternelle jeunesse du Mythe."
Atlantis 226 (1964): 59-84.
Boisse, Louis.
"Le Paysage et La Nature
Dans L'Oeuvre de Gustave Moreau."
Mercure de France 119 (1917):
417-428.
Breton, André.
"Gustave Moreau" (1961).
Le Surréalisme et la Peinture. Paris, 1965.
Cachin, Francoise.
"Monsieur Venus et l'Ange
Sodom, L'Androgyne
au Temps de Gustave Moreau."
*Nouvelle Revue de
Psychanalyse,* 7 (1973): 63-70.
Cartier, Jean-Albert.
"Gustave Moreau
Professeur à L'Ecole des Beaux-Arts."
Gazette des Beaux-Arts 61 (1963):
347-358.
Cazalis, H.
"Gustave Moreau et
Les Fables de La Fontaine."
Les Lettres et les Arts (1886): 58-67.
Charensol.
"Gustave Moreau, 1826-1898."
L'Art Vivant 31 (1926): 252-254.
Coquiot, Gustave.
Des Gloires Déboulonnées.
Paris, 1924: 101-120.
Coulonges, Henry.
"L'Atelier Gustave Moreau."
Jardin des Arts, 186 (1970): 32-39.
Cremona, Italo.
"Moreau Sconosciuto." *Circolare Sinistra*
4-5 (1955): 2-3, Ills. on pp. 15, 16,
18, 20, 22.
Dimier, Louis.
"L'Inspiration de Gustave Moreau."
Minerva 18 (1902): 261-279.
Dorra, Henri.
"The Guesser Guessed:
Gustave Moreau's 'Oedipus'."
Gazette des Beaux-Arts 81 (1973):
129-140.
Dreyfus, Albert.
"Gustave Moreau, 1826-1898."
Kunst für Alle 29 (1914) 169-178.
Duthuit, Georges.
"Vuillard and the poets of decadence."
Art News 53 (1954): 29-36, 62-63.
F. H.
"Gustave Moreau."
Kunst für Alle 17 (1902): 267-272.

Frongia, M. Luisa.
" 'Finito' e 'Non Finito'
Nell'Opera di Gustave Moreau."
Commentari 23 (1972): 139-151;
"Imiti classici nelle opere della
maturità di Gustave Moreau."
Storia dell'arte 13 (1972): 83-96.
Frongia, M. Luisa.
"Su alcune recenti interpretazioni
dell'opera di Gustave Moreau."
*Annali delle Facoltà di Lettere
Filosofia e Magistero,* Università Degli
Studi Di Cagliari,
Gallizzi (1973): 383-433.
Frantz, Henri.
"The New 'Gustave Moreau' Gallery."
Magazine of Art 24 (1900): pp. 97-104.
Geffroy, Gustave.
"L'Oeuvre de Gustave Moreau."
L'Oeuvre d'Art 1 (1900): 1-33,
plus eight plates.
Grojnowski, Daniel.
"Le Mystère Gustave Moreau."
Critique 19 (1963): 225-238.
Ironside, Robin.
"Burne-Jones and Gustave Moreau."
Horizon 1 (1940): 406-424.
Jenkins, Paul.
"Gustave Moreau:
Moot Grandfather of Abstraction."
Art News 60 (1961): 46-48, 57-59.
Jullian, Philippe.
"Il simbolismo: Gustave Moreau."
Arte Illustrata 2 (1969): 44-49.
Kaplan, Julius.
"Gustave Moreau's 'Jupiter and Semele'."
Art Quarterly 33 (1970): 393-414.
Lankheit, K.
"Gustave Moreau."
Das Kunstwerk 18 (1964): 29-30.
Larroumet, Gustave.
"M. Gustave Moreau et le Symbolisme
dans la Peinture."
Etudes de Litterature et d'Art,
Paris, 1896, pp. 253-298.
Derniers Portraits, Paris, 1904,
pp. 209-254.
Lejeaux, Jeanne.
"L'Oeuvre de Gustave Moreau."
Le Dessin 1 (1947): 14-24.
Loisel, L'Abbé.
"L'Inspiration chrétienne du peintre
Gustave Moreau."
Notes d'Art et d'Archéologie 24 (1912):
9-20, 31-42, 51-61, 76-86.
Mathieu, Pierre-Louis.
"Documents Inédits sur la
Jeunesse de Gustave Moreau
(1826-1857)."
*Bulletin de la Société de
l'Histoire de L'Art Francais* (1971):
259-279.

Mathieu, Pierre-Louis.
"Gustave Moreau amoureux,"
L'Oeil 224 (1974), pp. 28-33, 73.
Les Maîtres Artistes.
Paris, 1, 1901.
(Issue devoted to Moreau with
contributions by Léon D'Agenain.
"Le Rébus de G. Moreau." pp. 1-8;
J. K. Huysmans.
"Gustave Moreau." from *Certains.*
1889, pp. 8-9; Jacques Normand.
"Le Peintre 'Littéraire'."
pp. 9-10; Sar Péladan.
"Gustave Moreau." pp. 12-14;
André Mellerio.
"Gustave Moreau et le Modernisme."
p. 20; Jean, Lorrain.
"Le Musée Gustave Moreau." pp. 21-24;
Léon Thévenin.
"L'Esthétique de G. Moreau." pp. 24-31.
"Gustave Moreau et la Création du
Tableau." *L'Information d'Histoire de
L'Art* 10 (1965): 91-92.
Mauclair, Camille.
"Puvis de Chavannes and Gustave
Moreau."
International Quarterly
12 (1905): 240-254.
Meurville, Louis de.
"Gustave Moreau au Luxembourg."
Revue des Arts Decoratifs 19 (1899):
65-59.
Meyers, Jeffrey.
"Huysmans and Gustave Moreau."
Apollo (Jan. 1974): 39-44.
Michel, Edouard (ed.).
"Gustave Moreau et ses élèves.
Lettres d'Henri Evenepoël à son Père."
Mercure de France 161 (1923):
383-410.
Musée Gustave Moreau.
*Catalogue Sommaire des Peintures,
Dessins, Cartons et Aquarelles Exposés
dans les Galeries du Musée Gustave
Moreau.*
Paris, 1902.
1904 (reprinted in 1926).
1966.
1974.
Orliac, Antoine.
"Gustave Moreau."
Mercure de France (1926): 257-269.
Osler, P. G.
"Gustave Moreau:
Some Drawings from the
Italian Sojourn."
The National Gallery of Canada Bulletin
(1968): 20-28.
Péladan, Sâr.
"Gustave Moreau." *L'Ermitage.*
Paris, 1895, pp. 29-34.
Petibon, Mme.
"Gustave Moreau: Originalité de sa
Pensée et de son Oeuvre."
Bulletin des Musées de France
9 (1931): 207-209.
Phillips, Claude.
"Gustave Moreau,"
Magazine of Art 8 (1885): 228-233.
"The Fables of La Fontaine
by Gustave Moreau."
Magazine of Art 10 (1887): 101-103.

Pool, Phoebe.
"Degas and Moreau." *Burlington
Magazine*
105 (1963): 251-256.
Prache, Anne.
"Souvenirs d'Arthur Guéniot sur
Gustave Moreau et sur son enseignement
à l'Ecole des Beaux-Arts.
Gazette des Beaux-Arts 67 (1966):
229-240.
Ragon, Michel.
"Gustave Moreau." *Cimaise* 54 (1961):
12-21.
Reff, Theodore.
"More Unpublished Letters of Degas."
The Art Bulletin 51 (1969): 281-289.
Renan, Ary.
"Gustave Moreau."
Gazette des Beaux-Arts 33 (1886):
377-394 (1886): 35-51.
"Gustave Moreau."
Gazette des Beaux-Arts 21 (1899):
5-20, 189-204, 299-312;
22 (1899): 57-70, 414-432, 478-497.
Offprint, 1900, renumbered.
Restany, Pierre.
"Le Merveilleux et
Méconnu Gustave Moreau."
Planète 16 (1964): 81-95.
Rivier, Georges.
"L'Atelier Gustave Moreau et ses élèves."
Apollo (1946).
Roger-Marx, C.
"Gustave Moreau, seine Vorläufer,
seine Schule, seine Schüler."
Pan 3 (1897): 61-64.
Romanet, Fernand.
"Gustave Moreau."
La Revue Hebdomadaire 16: 310-330.
Rouart, Louis.
"Gustave Moreau."
L'Occident (1902): 152-162.
Rouault, Georges.
"Gustave Moreau."
Saisons 3 (1946-1947): 57-65.
"Gustave Moreau."
— A Propos de Son Centenaire."
Le Correspondant 1525 (1926):
141-143.
L'Art et les Artistes 66 (1926):
(Issue devoted to Moreau).
Souvenirs Intimes.
Paris, 1927, esp. pp. 1-51.
Rowe, L. E.
"A Water-Color by Gustave Moreau."
Rhode Island School of Design Bulletin
23 (1935): 34-36.
Schuré, Edouard.
Précurseurs et Révoltés. Paris, 1930
(first published 1904), for Moreau
see pp. 325-377.

Selz, Jean.
Modern Sculpture.
London, 1963, pp. 166, 178, 181.
Sturt, Charles R.
(pseud. for Charles Ricketts).
"A Note on Gustave Moreau."
The Dial 3 (1893): 10-16.
Trapp, Frank Anderson.
"The Atelier Gustave Moreau."
The Art Journal 22 (1962-1963): 92-95.
Von Holten, Ragnar.
"Oedipe et le Sphinx,
Gustave Moreau's genombrottsverk,"
Symbolister 3,
Tidskrift för Konstvetenskap
23 (1957): 36-50.
"Gustave Moreau Sculpteur."
Revue des Arts 4-5 (1959): 208-216.
"Le Développement du personnage de
Salomé à travers les dessins
de Gustave Moreau."
L'Oeil 79-80 (1961): 44-51, 72.
"Gustave Moreau und Die Sphinx."
Neusser Jahrbuch für Kunst,
Kulturgeschichte und Heimatkunde.
(1964): 11-15.
"Gustave Moreau Illustrateur de la
Fontaine."
L'Oeil 115-116 (1964):
20-27 and cover.
Weber, Gerhard.
"Some watercolors by Gustave Moreau."
The Connoisseur 167 (1968): 26-29.
Wright, Barbara.
"Gustave Moreau and Eugène Fromentin:
a reassessment of their relationship
in the light of new documentation."
The Connoisseur 180 (1972) 191.
White, Gleeson.
"The Pictures of Gustave Moreau."
The Pageant London, 1897, pp. 3-12.

Books and Articles that Refer to Moreau

Alvard, Julien.
Antagonisme. Paris, Musée des Arts
Décoratifs (1960): 10-11, 42-43.
Angrand, Pierre.
"L'Etat Mécène, période autoritaire
du Second Empire (1851-1860)."
Gazette des Beaux-Arts 71 (1968):
303-348, for Moreau see esp. pp.
309-310.
Ashbery, John.
"Paris Summer Notes."
Art International VI/8 (1961):
89-92, see esp. pp. 89-90.
Bacou, Roseline.
Odilon Redon. Geneva, 1965, 2 vols.,
for Moreau see Vol. I, pp. 254-258.
Basler, Adolphe and Kunstler, Charles.
La Peinture Indépendante en France.
Paris, 1929, for Moreau see Vol. I,
pp. 11, 14, 64; Vol. II, pp. 16, 17.
Bedouin, Jean-Louis.
"Trop D'Honneur."
Le Surréalisme, même 2 (1957): 11-104.

Bénédite, Léonce.
"Le Don Charles Hayem au Musée
du Luxembourg."
L'Oeuvre d'Art 141 (1899): 41-43.
La Peinture au XIXᵉ Siècle.
Paris, 1906, pp. 125-127.
Bengesco, M.
Melanges sur l'Art Français.
Paris, 1913, for Moreau see pp. 90-115.
Beraldi, Henri.
Les Graveurs du XIXᵉ Siècle.
Paris, 1890, Vol. 10, pp. 118-119.
Bergerat, Emile.
Les Chefs d'Oeuvre d'Art
à L'Exposition Universelle.
Paris, 1878, 2 vols, for Moreau
see Vol. I, pp. 156-159.
Blanche, Jacques-Emile.
Les Arts Plastiques La Troisième
République 1870 à Nos Jours.
Paris, 1931, for Moreau see pp. 28, 29,
32, 79, 95, 96, 111, 112, 113, 129, 131,
132, 134, 135.
Breton, Jules.
Nos Peintres du Siècle. Paris, 1899,
for Moreau see pp. 177-179, 212-217.
Bouyer, Raymond.
"Le Don Hayem au Musée du
Luxembourg."
Gazette des Beaux-Arts (Dec. 1, 1900):
593-598, for Moreau see pp. 594-596.
Cassou, J., Langui, E. and Pevsner, N.
The Sources of Modern Art.
London, 1962, for Moreau see
pp. 68, 126, 128, 148.
Castagnary, Jules-Antoine.
Salons. Paris, 1892, 2 vols, for Moreau
see Vol. I, pp. 196-202, 226-227,
367-368; Vol. II, pp. 227-228, 274.
Chastel, André, and Grand, Paule-Marie
in Breton, André.
L'Art Magique. Paris, 1957,
for Moreau see pp. 212-215.
Chesneau, Ernest.
Les Nations Rivales dans L'Art.
Paris, 1868,
for Moreau see pp. 179-208, 365.
L'Education de L'Artiste.
Paris, 1880, for Moreau see pp. 147, 193,
197-198, 218-219, 235-244.
Chevillard, Valbert.
Un Peintre Romantique Théodore
Chasseriau.
Paris, 1893, for Moreau see pp. 216-219.
Crespelle, J. P.
Les Maîtres de la Belle Epoque.
Paris, 1966, for Moreau
see esp. pp. 163-169.
Dorival, Bernard.
Les Etapes de la Peinture Française
Contemporaine. Vol. I and II,
for Moreau see Vol. II, *Le Fauvisme et*
le Cubisme 1905-1911.
Paris, 1943, esp. pp. 40-42.
Fels, Florent.
L'Art Vivant de 1900 à Nos Jours.
Geneva, 1950, pp. 36, 82, 151, 152,
153, 211.
Flat, Paul.
"Les Salons de 1897." *Revue Bleue*
20 (1897): 610-614.

Focillon, Henri.
La Peinture aux XIXᵉ et XXᵉ Siècles;
Du Réalisme à nos Jours. Paris, 1928.
Guiffrey, Jules.
"La Manufacture des Gobelins
à L'Exposition de 1900."
L'Exposition de Paris (1900). 3 vols,
for Moreau see Vol. I, pp. 268, 270.
Goncourt, Edmond and Jules de.
Journal Monaco, 1956, 22 vols.
Hautecoeur, Louis.
Littérature et Peinture en France
du XVIIᵉ au XXᵉ Siècle. Paris, 1942,
for Moreau see esp. pp. 108, 193-199.
Huneker, James.
Promenades of an Impressionist.
New York, 1910, pp. 348-356.
Huysmans, J. K.
A Rebours. Paris, 1884.
Certains. Paris, 1889, for Moreau
see esp. pp. 16-22.
L'Art Moderne. Paris, 1883,
pp. 135-138, 189, 194, 270.
Julian, Philippe.
Esthètes et Magiciens. Paris, 1969.
Robert de Montesquiou Un Prince 1900.
Paris, 1965, for Moreau
see esp. pp. 58, 76, 82-85, 115, 119,
148, 165, 166, 340.
Lahor, Jean.
"Sir Edward Burne-Jones."
La Revue de Paris 15, (1894): 102-122.
Lake, Carlton.
"Museum Treasure Hunt
Musée Gustave Moreau Paris."
The Christian Science Monitor 8
(1972): 8.
Lethève, Jacques.
La Vie Quotidienne des Artistes Français
au XIXᵉ Siècle. Paris, 1968,
for Moreau see pp. 16, 19, 53, 70, 76, 93.
Lorrain, Jean (pseud. for
Paul-Alexandre-Martin Duval).
Monsieur de Phocas Astarté. Paris, 1929,
for Moreau see esp. pp. 268-275.
Mauclair, Camille.
"The Gustave Moreau Museum in Paris,"
The Art Journal,
London (1905): 253-256.
Mauclair, Camille.
Les Etats de la Peinture
Francaise de 1850 a 1920.
Paris, 1921; for Moreau
see pp. 84-88.

Muther, Richard.
Ein Jahrhundert Französischer Malerei.
Berlin, 1901, for Moreau
see pp. 260-276.
Paris, Jean.
L'Espace et Le Regard. Paris, 1965,
for Moreau see pp. 37, 231-244, 247.
Pierre, José.
*Aquarelles de Filiger, Quelques Oeuvres
peu connues de Gustave Moreau et
Odilon Redon.* Paris, *L'Oeil,* Galerie
d'Art (1972): 18-24.
Praz, Mario.
The Romantic Agony.
Cleveland and New York, 1956
(Reprint from the 2nd ed. of 1951).
Proust, Marcel.
On Art and Literature 1896-1919.
New York, 1964, for Moreau see pp. 135,
308, 309, 413, and esp. 345-355.
Radiguet.
*Le Champ de Mars à Vol d'Oiseau;
Exposition Universelle 1867.*
Paris, 1868, for Moreau, see pp. 80-81.
Reverseau, Jean-Pierre.
"Pour une Etude du Thème de la Tête
Coupée dans la Littérature
et la Peinture dans la
Seconde Partie du XIXᵉ Siècle,"
Gazette des Beaux-Arts 80 (1972):
173-184, see esp. 175-177.
Sandstrom, Sven.
Le Monde imaginaire d'Odilon Redon.
Lund, 1955, for Moreau
see esp. pp. 45-52.
Savarus, Pierre de.
Dix Années d'Art. Paris, 1879,
for Moreau see pp. 85-96.
Serullaz, Maurice.
*French Drawings from Prud'hon to
Daumier.* Greenwich, Conn., 1966.
Symons, Arthur.
Studies in Seven Arts. London, 1906,
for Moreau see pp. 71-86.
Tabarant, A.
La Vie Artistique au Temps de Baudelaire.
Paris, 1943, for Moreau see esp. pp. 391,
417-418, 447.
Vachon, Marius.
Pour Devenir Un Artiste.
Paris, 1903, for Moreau see pp. 60, 109,
175, 213, 259, 264, 279-280.
Valery, Paul.
Degas Danse Dessin. Paris, 1965
(orig. publ. 1938),
for Moreau see pp. 63-66, 163.

Selected Exhibitions

1906 — Paris (Galerie Georges Petit),
Gustave Moreau
(Preface by Count Robert
de Montesquiou).
1934 — Paris (Exposition "Beaux-Arts"
et "La Gazette des Beaux-Arts),
Les Fauves. L'Atelier Gustave Moreau
(Preface by Louis Vauxcelles).
1949-1950, December-January — Paris
(Orangerie),
Eugène Carrière et Le Symbolisme
(Catalog by Michel Florisoone).
1956, April-May — Washington, D.C.
(The Corcoran Gallery of Art),
Visionaries and Dreamers
(Catalog by Henri Dorra).
1960, May-June — Cambridge, Mass.
(Busch-Reisinger Museum,
Harvard University),
*Gustave Moreau (1826-1898) and
Adolph Monticelli (1824-1886)
A Museum Course Exhibition.*
1961 — Paris (Louvre), *Gustave Moreau*
(Catalog by Ragnar von Holten).
1961, June 21-July 13 — Paris
(Les Deux Iles),
Autour de Gustave Moreau
1962, June-September — Marseille
(Musée Cantini),
Gustave Moreau et ses élèves
(Introduction by Jean Cassou).
1964, March-May — Munich
(Haus der Kunst) Secession,
*Europäische Kunst um olie
Jahrhundertwende,* Nos. 348-361.
1964, June-August — Neuss im Obertor
(Clemens-Sels Museum),
Gustave Moreau.
1964-1965, November-January — Tokyo
(National Museum of
Western Art), *Gustave Moreau.*
1964, August-September — Baden-Baden,
Gustave Moreau.
1966, July-August — Trieste
(Palazzo Costanzi),
Omaggio A Gustave Moreau.
1969, June-August — Turin
(Galleria Civica d'Arte Moderna),
*Il Sacro E Il Profano Nell'Arte
Dei Simbolisti,* Nos. 67-83.
1971, October-November — Tokyo
(Fujikawa Gallery), *Moreau and
Bourdelle.*
1972, June-July — London
(Hayward Gallery),
August-September — Liverpool
(Walker Art Gallery),
*French Symbolist Painters:
Moreau, Puvis de Chavannes, Redon
and Their Followers.* Nos. 138-190.
1972, October-November — Madrid
(Museo Espanol de Arte
Contemporaneo) *El Simbolismo
en La Pintura Francesa,* Nos. 348-361.
1974, February-April — Okayama,
Hiroshima, Tokyo
(Art Galleries of
The Tobu Department Store),
Gustave Moreau and His Students.

Photograph of Gustave Moreau
at about age fifty
▶

Designed in Los Angeles by
Rosalie Carlson.
All text set in 9 pt. Garamond by
Ad Compositors, Los Angeles.
The catalog is printed on Lustro Offset
Enamel by ColorGraphics, Inc.,
Los Angeles in a paperbound edition of
6100 and a clothbound edition of 2500.

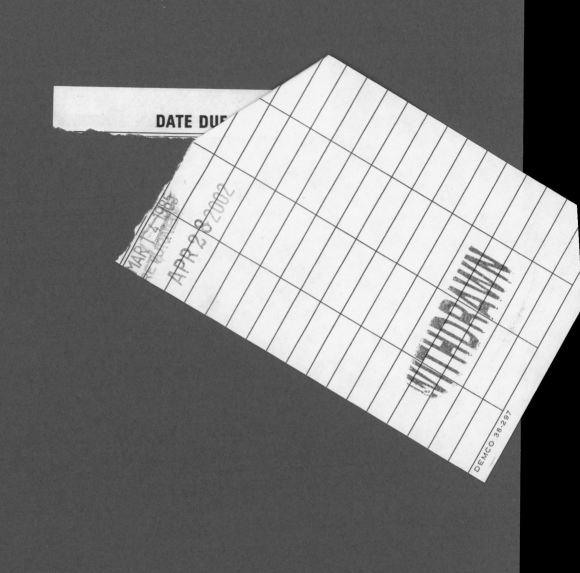